# Do It Right

If you are contemplating divorce—or are in the throes of one—this book is for you! It doesn't matter who started the proceedings—you or your wife—because this book is written to help you understand your legal rights and obligations.

# HOW TO DIVORCE
# YOUR WIFE

## Forden Athearn

LEISURE BOOKS ● NEW YORK CITY

A LEISURE BOOK

Published by
Nordon Publications, Inc.
Two Park Avenue
New York, N.Y. 10016

Library of Congress Cataloging in Publication Data

Athearn, Forden, 1928—
How to divorce your wife.

1. Divorce—Handbooks, manuals, etc.   I.   Title.
HQ814.A84        301.42'84
ISBN 0-385-08035-2
Library of Congress Catalog Card Number 75-14803

# Contents

# CHAPTER I

# For Men Only

## A. Why This Book

If you are contemplating divorce—or are in the throes of one—this book is for you! It doesn't matter who started the proceedings—you or your wife—because this book is written to help you understand your legal rights and obligations. It will forewarn you of some of the difficulties you may encounter.

This book is also written to enable you to have a better working relationship with your lawyer, not to act as a substitute for him. It is most certainly not a technical legal treatise on divorce. I have used few legal terms and have tried to express technical legal concepts in plain English. Although the laws vary from state to state, it is possible to discuss divorce laws generally and to provide you with a good idea of what it's all about. By the time you finish this book, you should have a working knowledge of what to expect from divorce—before, during, and after.

## B. What Is Divorce

Divorce is the legal termination of a valid marriage. Divorce is granted on grounds that theoretically have arisen subsequent to the marriage. In this respect it differs from an annulment. Annulment is the declaration by a court that a purported marriage was not valid to begin with by reason of some defect existing at the time it was entered into.

Most divorce judgments provide for more than just the termination of marriage. As incidents to divorce, the courts usually determine child custody and child support (if there are children), alimony, division of property, and other issues that may be necessary to give effect to the dissolution of a marriage.

The terms "divorce decree," "judgment of divorce," and "judgment of dissolution of marriage" all mean the same thing. The term used depends upon the state in which the divorce is granted. Some states, such as California, no longer use the word "divorce," but instead use the term "dissolution of marriage." Throughout this book I have used the word "divorce" to mean the legal termination of marriage, and the terms "divorce judgment" or simply "judgment" to mean the order the court makes in terminating the marriage.

Divorce must also be distinguished from legal separation. A judgment of legal separation gives the parties the right to live separate and apart. It may also determine all or some of the incidents of a divorce judgment, such as child custody, child support, alimony and property division; however, the parties are *not* free to remarry. This is the big difference.

## C. A Brief History of Divorce

The view any society takes of divorce is closely related to that society's ideal of marriage and the family. Even the most primitive societies seem to have had some method for terminating marriage. Since our American laws to a large extent are based upon English law, it is helpful to understand the development of the English laws and attitudes toward divorce.

Early Anglo-Saxon law provided for divorce in instances of adultery and desertion. It was not until the tenth or eleventh century that the Church of England was strong enough to impose its rules with respect to divorce.

Peter Lombard, Bishop of Paris, who lived sometime between 1100 and 1160, is generally credited with having originated the doctrine that marriage is a sacrament. From this doctrine came the concept that marriage is made in Heaven. Readily accepted by the Church, this doctrine established two things. The first was that the Church or ecclesiastical courts had exclusive power over marriage, divorce and related matters, a situation which continued in England until 1857. The second was that divorce became impossible to obtain. If marriage was made in Heaven, what power on earth could dissolve it? Though the ecclesiastical courts did not grant absolute divorces, they did grant judgments that today would be called "legal separations."

Men, even churchmen, are inventive creatures, and eventually the Church annulment became available as an instrument in terminating marriages. Annulments were granted by the Church courts on such grounds as a prior informal marriage, too close a relationship by marriage (affinity), or too close a relationship by blood (consanguinity). Consanguinity became expanded to include even remote blood relationships of the parties. It was upon his remote relationship by marriage that Henry VIII hoped to obtain a papal annulment from Queen Catherine of Aragon. The Pope's failure to grant Henry his annulment played a large part in the break of the English Church from Rome.

It might have been expected that with the break from Rome, the Church of England would have adopted a more liberal attitude toward divorce. Such expectancies, however, did not materialize. The ecclesiastical courts in England maintained jurisdiction over divorce until 1857, when jurisdiction was transferred to the civil courts, and adultery was authorized as the sole ground for divorce.

Another, though rarely used, device for obtaining a divorce in England, was the private bill through Parliament. It could be obtained only on the ground of adultery after the ecclesiastical court had granted a judicial separation, and usually after the wife's paramour had been successfully prosecuted in the criminal courts. As a practical matter, this bill was seldom available to the wife. It has some historic interest to us because the English example led to the practice of divorce by special legislative acts in various American states as late as the middle of the last century.

Ecclesiastical annulments and private legislative bills of divorce were only available to the very rich. The vast majority of people were forced to suffer the consequences of their earlier mistakes.

Since there were no ecclesiastical or Church courts in the American states, the state courts assumed jurisdiction over divorce. For the most part, the American courts adopted the rules of the English Church courts pertaining to divorce, and the various state legislatures passed statutes based upon the ecclesiastic laws. However, the American states were more liberal in passing statutes recognizing the possibility of complete divorce. In addition, many American states recognized grounds other than adultery.

Nevertheless, the attitudes of our American legislatures and courts are deeply rooted in religious and historical doctrines. Reform has been slow. In many states, grounds for divorce are restrictive. Until very recently, adultery was the only ground available in New York, a state generally thought to be modern and forward-thinking.

In some states, archaic defenses to divorce are still available. Take, for example, the defense of recrimination. This is the outrageous legal doctrine that states: When both parties have grounds for divorce, neither may have a divorce! All these impediments have as a prime, if unannounced, purpose—the discouragement of divorce.

As a result, the divorce laws on the books vary

considerably from the laws in action, the law as practiced by lawyers in courts for the benefit of their clients. For example, if judges and lawyers truly paid any attention to the defense of recrimination, there would be few divorces. Common sense tells us that seldom are all virtue and goodness on one side—and all blame on the other.

Such are the historical and religious roots of the institution of which you are about to avail yourself. Each of us is a product of that history. Our Judaic-Christian heritage has not only disapproved of divorce, it has sought to make it unobtainable. It is not unusual for us to feel a twinge of conscience when we act contrary to our heritage, just as we feel a sense of approval when we act in conformity with it.

Knowing the history of divorce can help us to cast off these painful twinges of guilt. Realizing that these doctrines, dogma, rules and laws governing divorce were made by men for men centuries ago, helps us to look upon divorce more objectively. These ancient ideas and rules bear little relation to the realities of today.

We are living in a period of greatly accelerated change. Even so, our laws of divorce are just now beginning to catch up with the twentieth century. Drastic changes have already been made in some states, and we can look forward to many more in the next few years. Current national statistics show that one marriage out of three will end in divorce. Obviously you are not alone.

Attitudes, as well as laws, are changing. It used to be that a man seeking a divorce worried about the reaction of his employer. A man in public office hesitated seeking re-election. A corporate executive feared facing his board of directors. Happily, these are no longer deterrents to divorce. The boss, the constituents and the board of directors are quite possibly divorced themselves—or thinking about it. Certainly they will not blame you or chastise you for merely divorcing.

## D. Making Up Your Mind

Making up your mind to obtain a divorce is not really a legal problem. Yet, a great many men and women come into a lawyer's office hoping desperately that he will make up their minds for them. The lawyer can't do this ethically or practically. Only you can make up your mind. Divorce is a personal decision. The reasons for marital discord which lead to divorce are as varied as the individuals themselves.

Human conduct, however, does tend to fall into certain categories. It may be that you want a divorce because you have found someone else, or that your wife wants a divorce because she has found someone else. It may be that your wife is flagrantly promiscuous, or that you are. It may be that your wife has an emotional or psychological problem which makes living with her difficult or impossible. Or, it may be that you have such problems.

Frequently a man and woman stay married to each other because their neuroses mesh. Early in my practice I handled the case of Audrey, a masochist, married to Bill, a sadist, who used to beat her regularly. For twenty-three years Audrey endured these beatings, hating the pain, but loving the feeling of suffering.

Audrey did reach a breaking point, and came to me for a divorce. The pain of the beatings finally outweighed the pain of getting a divorce.

Certainly this is an extreme case, but it illustrates the amount of suffering a human being will bear in order to avoid a divorce. Your problems may seem minor and inconsequential by comparison. You may wonder if you even *have* grounds for a divorce. If you haven't made the final determination, take the following test. It may help you to determine if you should proceed with a divorce or make another attempt to save your marriage.

## E. The Test

Ask yourself this question: Does the pain of remaining married for the rest of your life outweigh the temporary pain of getting a divorce?

I am not talking primarily about physical pain, but of the far more debilitating pain caused by an emotional upheaval. Divorce is often frightening to a man because he has absolutely no idea of what to expect. He fears giving up the known for the unknown. Even Shakespeare cautioned that it is better to "bear these ills we have than to fly to others that we know not of."

Change *is* awesome. Leaving the relative comfort of a home and a wife for an unknown hearth and uncertain companionship keeps many men stable as they go. This is not entirely a bad thing. It is often better to concentrate on what we have than to carelessly toss it aside.

In between irresponsible selfishness and misspent martyrdom is the answer to your question. If you have sincerely tried to make your marriage work and it hasn't, divorce is your salvation. But before you consult a lawyer, you may wish to talk with a priest, minister, rabbi, psychiatrist, or social worker who specializes in family problems. Ultimately, however, the decision must be yours.

## F. What to Do Before You Tell Her ✓

Once you have made the decision in favor of a divorce, the secret to success is *planning*. Carefully consider the personality and character of your wife, and be guided accordingly. If she is frugal, even-tempered, objective and not given to vindictiveness, you may not have to do any of the things that I am about to suggest. You should, however, carefully consider all of the following points:

### 1. *Close joint bank accounts*

If your wife is the type of woman who will take all of the money and leave you to pay the bills, go to the bank and close your joint accounts, whether they are savings or checking. Put the money in your name alone, but be prepared to account for it. I'm not suggesting that you hide this money or any other asset. What you are doing is taking defensive action. You are not seeking to hurt your wife.

## 2. *Take possession of the stocks, bonds and other securities that are readily salable*

Removing these assets from a joint safe-deposit box or desk drawer removes the temptation (to your wife) of running out and selling them. Again, put them in a safe place in your own name. You are not attempting to hide them; you are only taking defensive action.

## 3. *Close charge accounts*

Notify—in writing—all of your credit companies and all stores where you have charge accounts that you are undertaking a divorce and closing the account to your wife. Tell them that you will not be responsible for her charges after they receive this written notice. Again, this removes temptation. A distraught woman who wants to hurt her husband by charging great sums does not stop to consider that the money used to pay charges is going to come out of her share of the property or her alimony.

The most extreme incident of reckless charging that I have ever encountered was the case of Alan T., a middle-aged widower, comfortably established, with an excellent job. He remarried after his wife's death, but within eighteen months he knew that the marriage was wrong. He informed his wife that he wanted a divorce. At this news, she proceeded to run out and charge $37,000 worth of furs, clothing and jewelry. While Alan T. could not readily afford this kind of expenditure, he paid for these charges. It was the price he paid for hiding his embarrassment at being such a dupe. This may be an extreme example, but it is quite true.

4. *Make a complete list of the assets in your possession.*

After you have changed the bank accounts to your name and obtained possession of all the securities and other assets which are easily sold, make a list of them and their values. Remember, you are not trying to hide anything or be unfair to your wife. You are simply protecting yourself and—in the big picture—her.

Let me give you an example in reverse. I once represented a woman, Sylvia, whose husband, George, was an American diplomat serving in the capital of a foreign country. Making up her mind that the marriage was over, Sylvia left George and returned to this country. She immediately went to Washington, D.C., where all of the family assets were located, cleaned out the bank accounts and safe-deposit boxes, and came to San Francisco. At this point she consulted me. Timorously, she told me what she had done, fearing that it had been wrong. "Not at all," I replied. Later we accounted to George's lawyer to the last penny.

By taking this defensive action, Sylvia was assured of several things. First, George could not sit back and starve her out, as she had sufficient money upon which to live. Second, George was prevented from seizing the assets and hiding them. Third, it made settlement negotiations easier.

That case concluded successfully. Now, consider

a case whose conclusion was not as successful. Lillian announced to her husband, Ralph, that she wanted to end their twenty-one-year marriage. Instead of leaving it at that, she informed him that she had remet her high school sweetheart and was leaving California to join him in New York. Stunned, feeling completely rejected, Ralph moved out of the house. Once he was gone, Lillian took what furniture she wanted, and sold the rest. She also took an extremely valuable coin and stamp collection worth thousands of dollars. Although Ralph obtained a good property settlement, to this day he has never been satisfied with Lillian's accounting of what she took, nor of her purported appraisal of the coin and stamp collection. Had Ralph seen a lawyer right away, he would have been advised to take defensive action that would have prevented Lillian from leaving the state with some of his most cherished possessions.

Let me emphasize. I do *not* suggest you close bank accounts, charge accounts and take possession of the stocks in all cases. But if you are in doubt as to what she might do...?

## G. Consult a Lawyer

Contrary to what you see on television on "Perry Mason" or "Owen Marshall," lawyers don't work that way. Not all lawyers are knowledgeable about divorce, nor do all lawyers take divorce cases. Few lawyers even *like* to take divorce cases. The emotional involvement required in a divorce case is almost as hard on the lawyer as it is on the parties.

Also contrary to what you may think, lawyers do not make a fortune on divorce cases.

In selecting a lawyer, you should take many factors into consideration. The first is the man's reputation as a divorce lawyer. It may be that in your community there is a man or group of men who specialize in divorce. Find out who they are. Don't hesitate to see one or two of them to discuss your problems. You have to feel as right about your lawyer as you do about your doctor.

Another way to locate and rate a lawyer is to ask a recently divorced friend who his lawyer was and if he was satisfied with his lawyer's services. In listening to your friend's recommendation, remember that no one is entirely satisfied with his divorce, and many people tend to place the blame on their lawyer.

Many local bar associations have a lawyers' reference service. This service will be happy to give you the names of lawyers in your community who specialize in divorce cases. The lawyers' reference services are generally to be found in the yellow pages of your local telephone book.

## H. The Lawyer's Job

Once you have engaged a lawyer, tell him everything. Only by knowing *all* of the facts, favorable and unfavorable, can he help you. Tell him how you met your wife and how long you had known each other before marriage. Tell him your background and your wife's background. Tell him how long you've been married.

After you disclose these facts, then go into your

personal life. Describe as accurately as you can your personality and character. Describe your wife's personality and character. Tell your lawyer what you honestly feel went wrong with the marriage, and how each of you contributed to the problems. Tell him when you think the troubles started, and how. Tell him about your children, their personalities, the effect the divorce may have on them, and what their desires about custody are apt to be.

Telling your lawyer all about yourself, your wife and your marriage has a dual effect. First, it gives your lawyer the information he needs to protect you. Second, talking it all out helps you to clarify your thinking about your marriage.

After you've covered the personal side of the marriage, begin on the economic. Tell your lawyer where you work and how long you've worked there. Discuss your income, including bonuses, tips, profit-sharing plans, stock options and pension plans. If your wife works, discuss her income and her job record. List the family assets, their location and their value. Then describe what assets each of you may have inherited, whether before or during the marriage.

Be scrupulously truthful. By hiding assets and trying to "put one over" on your wife and her lawyer, you will damage your case. If you conceal assets and get caught, you may become involved in perjury charges. Even if your hidden assets are not immediately discovered, you are not home free. If, years later, your wife discovers that you did indeed conceal assets, she can bring a suit to set aside, on the ground of fraud, any agreement you had with her. She can even bring action against your estate after you have died and obtain the property which you hid.

After the discussion of property come the grounds for divorce. Here the conversation will be determined by your state's laws. Grounds, as we will discuss at length in Chapter IV, vary from state to state.

It is advisable in your first meeting with your lawyer to discuss his fees. Don't hesitate to ask questions. Many people think all lawyers' fees are exorbitant. Asking eliminates this fear. It also enables the lawyer to explain what he is going to do to earn this fee. The average person can understand what a doctor does because he's usually there when the doctor does it; but well over 90 per cent of a lawyer's work is done out of the presence of the client.

A lawyer's fee is based upon several factors. The first is the time involved. As Abraham Lincoln said, "All a lawyer has to sell is his time and advice." A divorce requires a set number of forms and procedures that simply take time to prepare. Client meetings take time. Phone calls take time. Court appearances take time. All these hours are figured in the fee.

If you question your lawyer's estimated fee, check with the local bar association. Many bar associations have, or had, a schedule of minimum fees, until the Department of Justice ruled that this was in violation of the Anti-Trust Laws. Nevertheless, your local bar association can probably give you an idea of what you can expect to be charged in the average divorce case.

It is impossible to predict the difficulty of each case. This is also a factor in fee setting. If your wife is unusually vindictive, impossible to negotiate with, hides assets and makes unreasonable demands, the job of your lawyer is going to be much more difficult. It is going to require greater skill on his part to achieve a fair result. For this he will expect to be compensated. His skill has been developed over a long period of time, and as the medical specialist commands a certain fee, so does the divorce specialist. This is why I urge you to discuss his fees. They are no mystery. Your lawyer is as anxious as you are to have an understanding. After all, this is how he makes his living.

## I. What Happens First

After you have had these preliminary discussions, your lawyer will explain what is expected of you on an immediate and temporary basis. If you have children, some provision must be made for their custody. Are they going to live with you or your wife? In most cases they will continue to live in the home where they are, and usually that will be with your wife.

If your children are going to be living with your wife, even on a temporary basis, you're going to have to contribute toward their support. The amount will be based upon their immediate needs and your ability to pay. Your income will be the prime factor in considering what is fair.

If your wife isn't working or isn't earning enough money to support herself on a temporary basis, you're going to have to make some contribution toward her support. Many domestic-relations courts have schedules, which are guidelines upon which awards of temporary child support and temporary alimony are based. The incomes of the husband and wife are the basis of these schedules.

Obviously you don't want your credit to be impaired simply because you're going through a divorce. Therefore, make a list of all your bills and arrange for their payment. Generally, it is better for you to assume payment of your family's debts than to expect your wife to pay them. This way you know that the debts are going to be paid. Correspondingly, if you assume payment on these debts, the alimony should be reduced.

You should also plan to make the mortgage-loan payments. Again, your assuming these obligations should be taken into consideration when the court awards temporary child support and temporary alimony.


## J. How to Tell Your Wife You Want a Divorce

Your lawyer will be able to give you some sound advice in this area. He has had years of experience. Is your wife volatile or calm? Can you reason with her, or does she have a closed mind? Can she be fair, or must everything be for her? Can you predict her reactions, or is she full of suprises? Once you have answered these questions, you can proceed. If you have determined that your wife is the type who will make a scene, is unreasonable and vindictive, then be sure you have already covered your bases by following the advice I gave you about your assets. With this type of woman, the shorter the statement, the better. Simply say that you are going to file, or have filed, for a divorce. Then walk out. Have your personal belongings already packed, and give her a note as to what plans you have made for her. It might even be better if you have already moved out before you tell her. You don't want to be tempted to hit her.

If your wife is the type who will be more or less reasonable (and take it quietly), you will be able to sit down and discuss the provisions you have made for her. Avoid arguments and recriminations by limiting your discussion to the essentials. The fact is, you've made up your mind for the divorce, and no purpose will be served by going back and ticking off the reasons. It's over. You can then sit down and tell her what you think are fair provisions for custody, child support, alimony and property division, and what steps you have taken in these matters.

## K. What to Do After You Tell Your Wife

I advise my clients to find a place to live temporarily, and move out. Many lawyers disagree with this advice, contending that it's the man's house too, so why should he leave? In my opinion, moving out lets your wife know that you mean business. The physical separation emphasizes your serious intent.

Moving out helps you in your own resolve, and also relieves tensions. If you are physically together in the same house, it may lead to arguments, blame-placing, quarreling, even violence. All of this is to be avoided. Even if you reconcile later, your physical separation will provide both of you with a cooling-off period and time to reflect upon what it is going to be like living separately. It may even be that this separation will make you decide you don't want the divorce after all.

If the house belonged to you before marriage and there are no children, then your wife should be the one to make the move. If she doesn't, you will have to remain and wait it out. But try to convince her that physical separation is important. Stress the fact that this is a very good way to test yourselves. Once she has gone, change the locks.

Some husbands, when they move out, practically denude the house. This is not only unfair, but totally unnecessary, particularly if there are children. Take your clothing, of course, and a few sheets and towels, maybe even a few cooking utensils that your wife can spare. If possible, consult your wife as to what you are taking. You don't want to run off with her favorite skillet when another would do. (Notice I am speaking of furnishings. I am not talking about the securities and other assets which I have already mentioned.) If there is extra furniture, take that, but don't remove the couch in the living room or the dining room table. If you have two television sets, take one. If you have a record collection, take half.

If you have children, your wife is going to continue to live in the home with them. They all have

31

a right to live comfortably. That is why it is to everyone's benefit if your wife approves of what you take. No matter what you select and what you leave, make a list for your files. Possessions, once out of sight, have a way of miraculously increasing in value. This list is your protection. Many wives have accused their husbands of running off with the "good stuff" and leaving them with the thrift shop specials.

Before you leave, tell your wife the financial arrangements you have made for her and the children. Be fair. Tell her that you have consulted a lawyer and that these figures are his. Tell her on what days you intend to send her money, such as the first and fifteenth day of each month, and then see to it that you send it on time. If you intend to take care of the mortgage, automobile and other household installment payments, tell her this, plus what other debts you intend to pay.

Explain to your wife why you've closed the charge accounts. Spare her the embarrassment of being told by the store that she no longer has an account there. If she objects, simply tell her that your lawyer told you to do it to protect both of you. Two households cannot live as cheaply as one. Until you have both experienced managing on less, the accounts should not be used.

Women worry about money. Knowing what your wife will be expected to live on will allow her to make plans. Be certain that she realizes her future debts are *hers*. You will no longer be responsible for any bills she may run up. You are not going to bail her out at the end of the month. Very often wives rush out and charge vast sums under the impression that the husband is *still* responsible.

Give your wife a copy of your list of assets. Tell her that you've closed the bank accounts and that you have possession of the stocks. You can explain to her that you have a perfect legal right to have these assets in your possession as long as you fully account for what you've done. At this time you should also give her the first support check.

## L. How to Tell the Children

Your approach will depend on the ages of the children. If they're very young, just tell them that Daddy is going away for a while. Tell them you love them very much, and you will be seeing them regularly, but probably not as often as you would like to.

If they're teen-agers, you can discuss the matter fully with them. Make sure that they understand you are divorcing their mother, not them. You love them as you always have, and your divorce does not change anything. You *must* convey this to your children by word and deed.

Teen-agers must understand that life carries its responsibilities. In informing them about your divorce, never speak disparagingly of your wife— their mother. Urge them to be as helpful as they can. Explain that since you won't be around as much, their mother is completely in charge. If they know you intend to back her discipline, they won't be so apt to try to "get away" with anything.

Children often feel that you want them to take

sides. This is why it is so necessary that you respect their mother and tell them you want them to respect her also. Let them know that they are not going to buy your love or affection by putting her down.

Children are very resilient. Soon the tears and trauma cease and they settle into the new living pattern. You can help this along by not talking about the divorce when you are with them. It is not up to you to explain all the intimate details of the divorce. As they grow older and ask questions about what happened, answer their questions without disparaging their mother. No matter *what* your problems were—or are—with her, they are certainly not *their* problems.

## M. How to Tell Others

Your boss is going to find out sooner or later, so tell him immediately. He will respect you more for your honesty. I don't recommend that you go into details with him. If necessary, you can say that you have made adequate arrangements for your wife and the children. If he presses for "the whole story," tell him without disparaging your wife. All disparagement will do is make him wonder about your judgment in marrying her in the first place. There is nothing wrong with making a mistake and admitting it. But to start placing the blame on your wife is unmanly—even if it was all her fault.

Your parents, brothers and sisters and other close relatives are also going to find out, so again, be the one to tell them. The depth of detail will depend upon your relationship with each. In general, it's best to avoid saying too much. The same rule applies as to your discussion of your wife. She was once their relative, and you should allow them to continue a relationship with her if they so desire.

If you have become close to certain members of your wife's family, you might want to talk to them about the divorce. You may want to assure them that you are going to do your very best to be fair with your wife, and continue your responsibility to—and for—your children. This will make it easier for them not to take sides and not to think unkindly of you. Keep your statement simple and to the point, always keeping in mind that old adage: "Blood is thicker than water." It's almost a certainty that whatever you say will be reported back to your wife.

If you find it necessary to tell your mutual friends, tell only those close to you. Again, the simple statement that you are divorcing and that you intend to be fair to your wife and support your children should be sufficient. You certainly don't want to tell them your wife's bad points. You never know who's going to get divorced next. Your old buddy Jim may finally dump Doris. He's always liked your wife. If he married her, it would certainly be a load off *your* wallet. But he's not going to be that interested if you tell him what a bitch she really is.

### N. How to Take Advantage of Women's Lib

Praadoxically, the Women's Liberation Movement has gone a long way in liberating men. Demand for equal work and equal pay has made alimony less popular, not only with the public, but with the courts and legislatures. Naturally, this has made divorce less of a financial burden on men.

Since the Women's Movement is fighting for social equality and the right to let women "do their own thing," men are feeling less guilty about leaving their wives and seeking a divorce. Women have given men a psychological lift. Now, when chastised by others for leaving your wife, you can say that equality, as well as freedom, works both ways. You want to do your own thing too!

# CHAPTER II

# The Emotional Trauma of Divorce: Men Have Feelings Too

## A. Regardless of Who Started the Divorce, Expect to Feel Emotional Trauma

Unfortunately, there seems to be no way to avoid the emotional upset and distress that accompany divorce. Even if you start the divorce, you cannot keep from being afflicted by tensions and trauma. If it is any consolation, I can assure you that millions of men have gone through what you are going through, and have survived. Most have come out better for it.

In the nineteen years that I have been handling divorces for both men and women, I have found that the trauma a client suffers depends, in large part, on what caused the divorce. Each case is different, certainly, but there are "categories of causes" which can be divided into five groups.

## B. The Man Who Has Been Cuckolded

No man is so far away from the jungle that he can passively accept his mate's running off with another. To many men, this is the epitome of emasculation. It leaves a man feeling rejcted, outraged, bitter and resentful. Even the knowledge that he is probably lucky to be rid of her is of small solace. His ego is damaged, and that is a difficult part of the body to repair.

When a man comes to me in this condition, seeking a divorce, the first thing I ask him to do is examine his wife's conduct. Only by a realistic and objective look at her can he begin to shake his feelings of rejection. What she did, she did to herself—not to him. He is still the determiner of his life, his future. If he continues to be defeated *(in absentia)* by her actions, he is allowing her to remain in his life.

If this has happened to you, beware of bitterness. It can cause you to resent all women because of one woman's actions. Just as you do not want to be damned by women who have had similar experiences with men, women don't want to be compared to your ex-wife. Let go. And this goes for the divorce proceedings. Don't fall into the trap of making a career out of your divorce litigation. A clean break is the quickest to mend. You will not hurt her by dragging it out. Have more regard for yourself and for your wallet.

I also advise the cuckolded man not to take his wife back—at least not right away. A man who quickly reopens his arms does it more to assuage his damaged ego than to profess his undying love. He is seeking more to restore his masculinity than to start over. One case that comes to mind is that of a prominent doctor whose wife was notoriously and flagrantly promiscuous. In fact, she was a tramp. The doctor took her back time and time again, not because he really wanted her as a wife—because she wasn't much of a wife—but because, consciously or subconsciously, it restored his ego and masculinity. Each time his psyche became more bruised. Eventually, he ended the torture by committing suicide.

One usually thinks of a doctor as a very "normal" human being, making a daily commitment to life. But in a divorce caused by a wife's infidelity, common sense often leaves with her. If the doctor had been able to examine himself, his marriage and his so-called "wife" and objectively and simply divorce her, this supreme tragedy would have been averted. As a doctor he should have looked at her clinically and realized that she had serious psychological problems which prevented her from acting in any capacity as a wife, or participating in any kind of genuine marriage. Promiscuity is the result of a missing link within the person who is engaging in it. It is not a barometer of the other partner's sexual prowess.

If your wife has walked out on you—let her go. Conclude the divorce as rapidly as possible. Remain objective, fair and detached. Your actions will completely astound her. As a matter of fact, letting go with a quick, clean break is the ultimate victory!

Of course, to forget and move on is easy to say—

hard to do. Just keep telling yourself that you are far better off without her—and you are! Which reminds me of a line in Kipling's poem "The Young British Soldier":

> If the wife should go wrong with a comrade, be loth
> To shoot when you catch 'em—you'll swing, on my
>   oath!—
> Make 'im take 'er and keep 'er: that's Hell for them both,
> An' you're shut of the curse of a soldier.

## C. The Man Whose Wife Asks for the Divorce

Statistically, it is usually the woman who files for the divorce. The man's most common emotional reaction to this is a feeling of rejection. Bitterness and resentment creep in. Frequently, his resentment takes the form of heated argument over the property division, regardless of the values involved.

I recall the case of Peggy and Herb A. She simply wanted "out," but he was so resentful and bitter that he fought her every inch of the way. His most irrational and absurd moment came when he instructed his high-priced lawyer to fight for the "custody" of two antique mandolin picks the couple had purchased together in Spain. The lawyer's time consumed in arguing over the award of the mandolin picks far exceeded their value. It finally came to the point that Herb's lawyer said he would *buy* him another set of antique mandolin picks. And with the attorney's fees he collected, he could well afford it.

It doesn't actually matter who started the divorce. If it was your wife—so much the better. She is probably doing what you should have done years ago. You, like so many men, have probably wanted the divorce and have subconsciously been acting in a way to bring it about. Don't punish her now for her overt honesty.

## D. The Man Wants "Out" Because of Another Woman

If you have fallen in love with another woman and she is pressing you to get a divorce, expect to feel tremendous guilt. This is not an uncommon situation. Guilt keeps more marriages together than the church. A client of mine, Robert W., is a perfect example. Bob, when he came to me, had not lived with his wife for years. He had moved out at least four years before and lived with his mistress, who really was a lovely woman. Bob wanted desperately to marry her, but his overwhelming sense of guilt made him delay the divorce year after year after year. His guilt feelings kept him prisoner to a marriage situation that scarcely existed and caused him to waste many years that he could have spent in a happy second marriage.

If you are a man sincerely in love with another woman, then divorce your wife and marry her. This is a much more honest posture than keeping the three of you locked in an ignominious state. There are few things a man can successfully hide from his wife; another woman is *not* one of them.

After you have made up your mind to obtain a divorce, do it as quickly as possible. Be fair in the property division, but take your lawyer's advice. A sense of guilt can also cause a man to mortgage his future by agreeing to unreasonable monetary demands. Another word of caution: Give yourself a breather before you jump into another marriage. If the other woman truly loves you, she'll understand. If she doesn't, I'd suggest even a *longer* waiting period. It's *your* life. Why jump from the frying pan into the fire? Or as Confucius says: "Man who marry for second time did not deserve to lose first wife."

## E. The Man Who Simply Wants "Out" ✕

When a man finds himself in this category, he frequently feels enormous guilt because he doesn't have a good, unchallengeable reason for wanting "out" of the marriage. His wife may be a good mother, fine cook, faithful and attractive. Still, he feels trapped, stifled, cornered. He knows there is more to life than what he has, and he fervently wants to find it. But he can't find it with the wife he has.

Recently I handled the case of Walter H., who described his wife as an intelligent, attractive woman who had kept her figure. She ran a well-ordered home and took excellent care of their children. But to him she had become a near stranger. They were two individuals living together, but on different planes. He was becoming more detached as he built up a fantasy world full of excitement and adventure. He finally reached a point where he felt he would have a breakdown if he spent the rest of his life in this vacuum.

At this point Walter came to me. He told me of his agony, how he had spent hundreds of nights asking himself questions. Was he being selfish? Was he being cruel? Would he suffer regrets ever after? Over and over he asked himself the same questions. And over and over he found he had no answers. Divorce, I agreed with him, was the solution.

When he began to discuss the particulars of a settlement, his over-powering guilt made him propose a property settlement that would have kept him financially strapped for the rest of his life. I told Walter what I tell all my male clients who want to publicly purge themselves: Divorce is a remedy—*not* a punishment. There is no law on the books that says a man has to stay in a miserable condition because he made a wild promise in his twenties to love, honor and cleave till death did him in. There is also no reason why he has to give away all his earthly possessions to buy himself a bit of freedom. It is not wrong to seek happiness. It is not wrong to want "out."

Then, there's the case of Marvin L., who had four sons. For years he and his wife had not gotten along. Both had a long history of extramarital affairs. Unfaithfulness was their panacea for boredom. Yet Marvin could not bring himself to sue for divorce. He carried a tremendous load of guilt directly traceable to his upbringing. To him, the act of adultery was more acceptable than the act of divorce.

When a man comes to me in this condition, I try to make him examine his early life and look at these inherited values for what they are: someone else's code of conduct. What worked for our ancestors is not necessarily going to work for us.

As far as his four sons are concerned, to my way of thinking, flagrant promiscuity is far more destructive than an honest divorce. Children can and do adjust to divorce, but finding their parents engaging in a string of tawdry liaisons could not only be embarrassing, but permanently damaging. More lives are ruined by a misplaced sense of guilt than any other emotion I can name.

## F. The Mutual Divorce

Embitterment and a sense of lost opportunities are the emotions evoked by the mutual divorce. When a husband and wife jointly agree to part, they often look at each other and say simply, "So it has come to this." It is a devastating emotion to learn that neither of you cares any longer. The shared hopes and plans, moments of romantic delight, have all come to nothing. It was a false start, a play with no ending, a void.

The advice I offer in such cases is to look at divorce—not as an ending but as a beginning. There are so few times in life that you can actually "start over" with a brand-new deal. Divorce is one of them. Stop the regretting—it won't help you to build a new life. Chalk it all up to experience, and resolve that the remainder of your life is going to be happier. You've found out in time to begin again.

44

## G. The Foolish Reactions to Divorce that Are Self-Destructive

When the human body suffers a psychological upheaval—which divorce is—the reactions are often physical as well as emotional. Just making the decision is a hard battle that leaves your nervous system battered and bruised. In this condition, a man will do any number of things that are not only contrary to his nature, but are harmful—and damned foolish! Following is a list of the most common reactions you should be on guard against.

### 1. *Excessive drinking*

When you are separated or divorced, you are alone. You may suddenly find yourself in a dingy little apartment which you can't stand. Your laundry piles up, the bed is unmade, the sink is full of dirty dishes. In this situation, it is easy for a man to reach for the bottle as a temporary solace. It's quick, it's easy. Unfortunately, it adds to your vulnerability instead of strengthening your stand. It clouds your vision and, if continued over a long period of time, destroys the good things. The danger of drinking excessively is that one never thinks one is—until it's too late.

### 2. *Letting your job or business go to pieces*

When a man is upset, his job performance suffers. This is certainly not a new or startling statement. But the adverse effects of the unsettlement of divorce can make a man almost hate his job. As he drags his body out of bed each morning, he may be mumbling to himself, "Why should I work my head off just so I can pay her each month? What future is in it for me? Why don't I just enjoy myself more and knock off earlier?"

It's not difficult to see where such thinking leads. Deluding oneself with a false sense of pity is dangerous. Your job—instead of being your enemy—should be your friend. Embrace it. This is a time to work harder, not slough off. You are in total control of your future. You may want to marry again. Why throw everything away just to "show her"?

### 3. *Wenching*

There is nothing wrong with "wenching" as such. But with the new freedom of divorce, a man may suddenly find himself involved with the type of woman with whom he ordinarily would not be caught dead. This becomes a blow to his already bruised ego. You may also lower yourself in the estimation of your friends and business associates.

There is also a chancy element in your decision to "screw everything that comes along." You're liable to get "everything that comes along"—including VD. There is most certainly no shortage of available bed partners who will "pass the test." So when you wench, do it with a little style.

## 4. *Talking too much about your divorce and related problems*

Usually it is the woman who talks too much about her divorce, accusing her husband of all kinds of cruelties and misdeeds. However, men are not blameless in this conduct. Men, too, often wage a campaign to convince the world of the lousy deal they got. This is especially true of the man who is forced to pay what he considers more than a "fair share" of his income. It is also true of the man whose wife left him for someone else.

Some men who "tell all" about their ex-wives claim they are doing it in self-defense. They say their wives went running around telling friends, neighbors and acquaintances what a son of a bitch they are, and they want to set the record straight. This is rationalization. If a man in this position would just hold his tongue and not retaliate, he would automatically become the "long suffering" good guy. Isn't this what you're after?

## 5. *Brooding*

Divorce carries more than its share of mental anguish. It involves, as we have discussed, the element of choice. And with choice comes responsibility. If a man has had a difficult decision to make, he worries about it. He tortures himself mercilessly. Did he do right? Could he have done things differently? What permanent damage has he done?

This sort of heedless worry soon turns to

47

brooding. And all brooding does is prevent you from getting on with life and building a sound future. No one enjoys the company of a moody person. You will not only cut yourself off from those you care about, but you will discourage new friendships.

### 6. *Hiding or squandering assets*

When a man starts hiding assets so his wife won't be able to find them, he must then lie to his wife, her lawyer, his lawyer, and the court. If he gets caught, he stands the chance of losing all of those assets.

If you are contemplating this, remember: You have to live with yourself. Why walk around with more guilt feelings? Your lawyer is your best ally when it comes to retaining your assets. He'll help you—legally—to keep the maximum.

The opposite of the man who clutches his money is the man who squanders. He reasons that he might as well spend it on himself. If he doesn't the court will give it all to her. This, of course, is nonsense. No court is going to nail a man to a financial cross. Flagrantly splashing your money around may make a few good times, but come Monday morning, it's back to reality. You are far ahead of the game if you judiciously hold on to what you have.

### 7. *Fleeing the state*

Flight has always been a remedy for fear and confusion. A confused, unhappy man in the throes of a divorce will often contemplate fleeing the state to avoid paying alimony and child support. The problem is, of course, that he leaves everything behind. If he has children, he won't be able to see them. If he has family, relatives or friends, it will be impossible to see them. If he has a good job or a business, he will be sacrificing it. Flight just isn't worth it. Legally you are still responsible, and the law follows you wherever you go. Divorce never killed anyone that I know of, so just stay put and work it all out.

### 8. *Hating and blaming all women*

In my bachelor days I disliked dating divorcees who talked about nothing but their divorce, their problems with their ex-husband, and their suffering. The reverse is also true. The women you date don't want to hear about your divorce, your problems, and what a bitch your "ex" is.

There is another lesson here. All women are not alike, and it is unfair to lump them together as "grasping, deceitful, untrustworthy" females. When you blame all women, you sound like a jerk. You also lessen your chances of finding the right woman for you. Each woman is a unique creature—albeit confusing—and should be treated as such.

### 9. *Jumping into an inappropriate lifestyle*

A man severed from home and family often feels that *now* is the time to do all the things he has been kept from doing. *Now* he can live on a houseboat, grow a beard and read Zen. *Now* he can sell his business, buy a motorcycle and see America. *Now* he can chuck his professorship, join a commune and raise organic vegetables. *Now!*

We all have dreams, fantasies, in which we are far happier than we are now. In these make-believe lives we are Picasso or Sir Francis Drake or Paul Newman. We are rich. We are famous. We are adventure seekers. Women crave our bodies. Life opens all her mysteries to us. But we should know these temptresses for what they are—pleasant time-wasters. Unfortunately, many a newly divorced man does not. His fantasies take over, cloud his judgment, and scream: *YES*—now *IS* the time!

Taken individually, there is actually nothing wrong with any of these dreams. Some could even become happy realities. What is wrong is for a man, in a fit of post-divorce craziness, to toss aside what is very real—for what is at this moment very unreal. Time is the great ally. Wait. Take your life a step at a time. Your dreams must be able to take place in the real world, or keep them as dreams. Don't risk the added devastating embarrassment of making an ass of yourself.

### 10. *Becoming a doormat for your wife*

There is a certain kind of man who lets a woman walk all over him. When this type of man goes through a divorce, he becomes more flattened than ever. He acts cowed and beaten. He gives in on every count and accedes to unfair demands.

Obviously, this type of behavior does neither of them any good. The more the man gives in, the more the wife demands. If you have a nagging feeling that this describes you, then heed your lawyer's advice.

Let him do the negotiating for you. Refuse to discuss the divorce with your wife.

Some women are plain and simple "ballcutters." This type of woman rules certain men by playing on their insecurities, threatening the whole man. For you to have further contact with such a woman is to run the risk of enlarging your inferiority complex, jeopardizing your work effectiveness, and ultimately losing your male potency. Enough said.

## 11. *Entertaining schemes to "do away with her"*

Men have said to me, "I have Mafia connections, you know. I can have my wife done away with for less than it's going to cost me in alimony." Of course, such a man doesn't mean it. The statement simply shows the depths of his emotional disturbance. Even allowing such thoughts to exist is self-defeating. They ruin your ability to be objective in settling your affairs with your wife.

Making rash statements aloud can also be dangerous. If overheard, people begin to question your stability. A threatening statement could also be used against you in court. You have suggested that you possess a violent nature. You have opened a Pandora's box of speculation. And if indeed something "mysterious" should happen to your wife, you would be a prime suspect.

In essence, you have "done away" with your wife—you've divorced her. Entertaining any thoughts about her—threatening or otherwise—keeps her very much a part of you. Forget it. Let her go. Whatever you are paying is money well spent.

## H. The Tricks Your Wife May Pull to Get You Back

Let us assume that you have examined your emotions as objectively as possible. You have made up your mind to obtain a divorce. You have been forewarned of some of the self-destructive conduct that tempts the man in divorce. Let us also assume that you have consulted a lawyer and gained an idea of your legal rights and obligations. You have told your wife that you want a divorce, and you've moved out. You may even have started the divorce proceedings.

Now—suppose that your wife decides she wants you back! She may come right out and tell you. Hopefully, you can deal with that. But, more often than not, a woman who wants her husband back begins a subtle (sometimes not so subtle) campaign to convince him of the error of his ways. The devices and tactics she uses will vary—depending upon her estimate of the man's character and personality. Basically, if your wife wants you, you can expect one (or all) of the following methods to be used. Good luck!

### 1. *Guilt*

Back to this again! Well, if you feel guilty about your divorce, for one reason or another, the clever wife will know this and you can count on her using it for all it's worth. Take the case of William S. William met Shirley in New York on a business trip, married her three months later, and brought her to San Francisco, where his business and home were.

William had been smitten by Shirley's charms and, because he knew her such a short time, was unaware that under the charm were serious emotional instabilities. The marriage was disastrous. Eighteen months later, William walked out and got a divorce.

Ah, but that was not the end of the story! Shirley is a cunning woman, and she is still very much a part of William's life. Playing on his guilt, she insists that he take her out twice a month. After all, she whines, "You brought me clear out to California, where I don't know anybody." She calls him when her car breaks down. She drops by his office at lunchtime. She picks up his shirts at the laundry and drops them by his apartment. She just keeps heaping on the guilt. Will she get him back? There's a good chance of it. Yet William knows—and repeats it to me—that if he does remarry her, he will be seeking another divorce in three months. Is this any way to live a life? Hell, no! And to hell with guilt!

## 2. Children

How many times have I heard both partners in a marriage say that they went back "for the sake of the children." The man or the wife who uses this as an excuse is only kidding himself or herself and damaging the children in the bargain. Psychiatrists are largely agreed that a bad marriage is harder on children than a divorce.

A case that immediately comes to mind is Wendell V. Wendell was the West Coast head of a large company, and he had to travel a great deal. He had a veritable stable of girl friends and was not very secretive or careful about who knew it. His teen-age daughter and son knew before his wife, Patricia, did. Wendell had not slept with Patricia in five years, but Patricia convinced him to stay in the marriage "for the sake of the children." She had learned of the other women, but her plan was to "hang in there" and outlast them. Wendell was convinced that Patricia was right about keeping the marriage together. So what did he do? When he wasn't on the road with one of his girl friends, he was locked up in his study. Here he would look at nude pictures of himself with his girl friends while listening to tape recordings of them having intercourse. All the while he would masturbate.

It's not hard to imagine that Wendell became sexually abnormal. His actions became more bizarre. Patricia, who kept him there "for the sake of the children," was robbed of her chance to find another husband and build a normal life. The children became emotionally disturbed, and later required psychiatric help.

One final thought for you to consider. Few things grow faster than children. They will be grown and gone before you know it. Then you will be left sitting across the room from a wife you haven't really liked or even talked to in years. You will both be bitter. Going back "for the sake of the children" may seem like a noble gesture. However, it could also be mental suicide.

### 3. *Helplessness*

One of the strongest ties a man has to his wife, or

indeed one person to another, is the feeling of being needed. When we feel that we are no longer needed, we are frequently in for a psychological trauma. A plea from an ex-wife that she needs you and can't get along without you, is a hard appeal to reject. It grabs you by your masculinity. If indeed she really does need you, maybe you can't reject this ultimate appeal. All of us need to be needed. But just remember that this can often be a form of slavery where the needy enslave the needed.

### 4. *The good times*

If you are romantic, her appeal to what you "meant to each other" may do the trick. Frankly, if it works, maybe you shouldn't be getting a divorce after all. Perhaps you should consider a reconciliation. However, if you know that the bad times outweighed the good times, you had better concentrate on remembering those. You can't have a party every night of the week.

### 5. *Threats*

The vengeful female who threatens to "ruin you" if you don't come back, has watched too many movies. If she is threatening you with financial ruin, she can't do it. The law protects your rights as well as it protects hers. It protects your property and it sets reasonable standards by which you will have to support your wife and children.

Blackmail, of course, is a different problem. If you have done something illegal, such as cheat on your income tax and your wife knows about it, by all means tell your lawyer the whole story. Let him handle what has to be done. If you allow your wife to blackmail you, you are mortgaging your future.

If your wife is threatening to expose your affairs with other women, nobody really cares. Her disclosures are not going to hurt you in your job, business or community. She simply makes a pitiful spectacle of herself. You might gently remind her of this.

I have known many women to threaten to expose their ex-husbands as acting or latent homosexuals. Fortunately, our level of sophistication makes this a self-destructive threat. Even the medical profession no longer lists homosexuality as a "disease." If a woman has been physically "rejected" in her marriage, pointing a finger at her husband and exclaiming "homo" seems to transfer the fault from her to him. She rationalizes that their lack of sexual activity is his problem, not hers. The truth is usually that the husband is only tired of *her,* not all women. So if your wife is waving this ineffectual flag in front of you, ignore it. Leave her to her venom.

Remember, all these tactics to get you back might not be because she wants you for yourself. Divorce has damaged her feminine ego. She may find that it's harder to get along than she had anticipated. The men she envisioned taking her out to dinner may not have materialized. Her bills are piling up. The roof leaks, and she's having trouble with the kids. Suddenly, you look like Prince Charming. Of course, she wants you back!

# I. Getting Her Back

Or the counterpart of all this may have happened to you. The sight of her sitting demurely across the table from you in your lawyer's office may tug at your very guts. Her faults may dim at the remembrance of her deep-dish apple pie. Climbing into a solitary bed on more nights than you *thought* you would, could make her look soft and desirable. If indeed you do decide you want her, once more, for your very own, I recommend four possible approaches:

## 1. *The religious approach*

If religion is important in your life, discuss your problems with your minister, priest or rabbi. Most clergymen have had training in handling marital problems. Since they have "heard it all before," they have a wealth of wisdom upon which to draw. When he has heard your complete story, he may suggest carrying your cause himself. What better Cupid's messenger than a man of the cloth!

## 2. *The psychiatric approach*

If you can afford to talk about your problems with a psychiatrist, psychotherapist or psychologist—do. But be careful in your selection. There are many self-styled "counselors" in the field who could themselves use psychiatric help. I suggest that you consult your family doctor and get his recommendation.

Although psychiatrists, psychotherapists and psychologists can be very helpful, they're not miracle workers. It is often possible to return a marriage to a good state it once had and lost—but it is impossible to create a good marriage when one never existed. What a competent therapist can do is help you gain insight into yourself and why the marriage failed in the first place. With this knowledge, you may be able to take steps to reconstitute your marriage.

### 3. *Courts of conciliation and other public agencies*

Many states, such as New York and California, have Courts of Conciliation services or public agencies which advise husbands and wives in their marital problems. They use many of the same techniques that psychiatric workers use. One exception, of course, is that these services are usually free. Again, remember that these social workers are not miracle workers. They can only guide and advise. They cannot wave a magic wand and make a marriage work.

### 4. *The hearty application of "humble pie"*

If, by a process of self-analysis, you believe that you have arrived at some answers to yourself, your wife and your marriage, knock on her door and tell her that you want to try again. From there on, it's up to you both. Good luck!

# CHAPTER III

# Jurisdiction: The Out-of-State Quickie, or How to Waste Your Money

## A. Going Off to El Salvador

Flying off to El Salvador or Ensenada or Nevada to obtain a divorce may seem romantic in the movies, but like so many situations on the silver screen, it is not practical or realistic, because in many cases the divorce is not valid. Why do so many otherwise rational people consider dashing off to do the divorce deed elsewhere? One reason is because divorce puts you emotionally off balance.

One of the unsung tasks of the lawyer is restoring—or trying to restore—logic in his clients' minds. Often an unhappily married man will dwell on divorce for years before he decides to take the step. Once this man has made up his mind, he wants action. Right now. Fast. He wants to end twenty years of suffering in twenty minutes.

Divorce takes *time*. In some states, an inordinate

amount of time. This is frustrating and everyone in the field is aware of it, except those seeking the divorce. They often feel it is the lawyer's fault and will complain, cajole and threaten to leave the state. This is especially true of the married man who has a girl friend waiting in the wings. It is part of the lawyer's job to patiently and thoroughly explain the problem of jurisdiction. Jurisdiction is a complicated and highly technical subject even for the lawyer, but there is no reason why the client should not at least be aware of the problems and principles involved.

## B. Where Is it Safe to Get a Divorce?

The best and safest place to get a divorce is the courthouse of the county in which you live. This is not obstinacy on the part of the law. Each state is concerned about its citizens. Each state protects and cares for its citizens. Therefore the state has the right and the obligation to decide the divorce, to make the necessary divorce rules for its citizens, to protect the children of the marriage, the property rights of each party, and the support rights of each, and their parental rights.

If a husband and father were allowed to run off and divorce elsewhere at will, the home state would be responsible to care for that man's wife and children if he failed to do so. This is unfair to everyone concerned—most particularly the taxpayer left to assume the man's obligations. As a hedge against such practices, all states except two have a resident requirement for divorce that may vary from six weeks to a year. The residence requirement simply provides that you must have been a good-faith resident of the state for a certain length of time before the state will act to grant you a divorce.

## C. Is It Impossible to Divorce in Another State?

No, it is not impossible. In some cases it is not only possible but advisable. If you live in a state whose grounds for divorce are so archaic you fear you will never be free, then by all means consider residence elsewhere. But consult a lawyer in your home state first, before you pull up stakes. The procedure is not simple.

## D. What Happens When You Divorce Outside Your State?

As I said, each state has jurisdiction over its citizens. Nevertheless, the United States Constitution requires that each state give full faith and credit to the judgments of its sister state. This does *not* mean you can go to another state, get a divorce and return home a free man. Your home state still has some say about your actions.

This can best be illustrated by a famous case involving two couples from North Carolina. William left his wife, Carrie, and his friend Lillie left her husband, Thomas. William and Lillie then journeyed from North Carolina to Nevada, where they established residence by remaining six weeks. At the end of that time each got a divorce, married, and returned to North Carolina. Once across the border, they were prosecuted and convicted of bigamy.

The North Carolina Court held that since neither Carrie nor Thomas (the deserted parties) had been served with the divorce papers in Nevada, their respective divorces were not valid. You may not, the court said, leave the state for the sole purpose of obtaining a divorce and force your home state to recognize it. When appealed to the United States Supreme Court, the decision was upheld. North Carolina did not, under these circumstances, have to recognize the out-of-state divorce of its citizens, despite the full faith and credit requirement of the Constitution.

In another celebrated case, Margaret left her husband, Edward, in Massachusetts and moved with her children to Florida. Margaret got a job and enrolled her children in school. After she had lived there the required ninety days, she filed for divorce. Edward hired a lawyer in Florida to represent him, and the lawyer filed an answer to Margaret's complaint for divorce. At the time of the proceedings in Florida, Edward appeared and testified but did not challenge Margaret's claim to be a resident of Florida. Margaret got her divorce, married another man, Philip, and returned to Massachusetts.

When the newlyweds entered Massachusetts, Edward sued for custody of the children, claiming the divorce was not valid, as Margaret had not been a Florida resident. In this case, the Supreme Court upheld Margaret's divorce because Edward had appeared in Florida and had not challenged her residence during the Florida proceedings.

In an attempt to resolve these confused cases, many states have now adopted the *Uniform Divorce Recognition Act*. This Act provides that a divorce obtained in another jurisdiction shall not be recognized in the home state if both parties to the marriage were residents of the home state at the time the divorce was commenced.

Added to this is the problem of alimony, child support, property division and child custody. Who decides these issues if you go out of state? Your home state may, or the state where your wife has chosen to reside may decide them. This situation can best be illustrated by the much-publicized Vanderbilt case.

Patricia and Cornelius Vanderbilt, Jr., separated while they were living in California. Patricia moved to New York and Cornelius to Nevada, where he filed for and obtained a divorce. Patricia did not hire a lawyer there nor did she appear in Nevada. Later, however, she brought an action in New York for support. Cornelius contended that the Nevada divorce terminated his support obligation. Not so. When taken to the Supreme Court, the ruling was that, since Patricia was not subject to the jurisdiction of the Nevada Court, the Nevada Court could not cut off her right to support.

Confusing? Indeed so. That's why my advice is to get a hometown divorce with all loose ends properly tied.

To recapitulate the dangers of an out-of-state divorce:

1. Your home state might not recognize your out-of-state divorce when you return.
2. Your home state may still decide the issue of

child custody.

3. Your home state may still require you to pay alimony and child support according to its laws.
4. Your home state may still proceed to divide your property pursuant to its laws.

What have you gained? A questionable divorce.

### E. How to Get a Valid Out-of-State Divorce

Ah, you say, but you *must* go to another state for a divorce. You simply can't wait for your home state to come 'round. Then, here is what you must do!

*First:* Know the residence requirement of the state to which you are going. It varies. For example, it is six weeks in Florida and Idaho as well as Nevada.

*Second:* Your wife must appear in the new state. She can appear in person, through her lawyer or by signing a written appearance. If she doesn't, she can raise the issue of the validity of your divorce and the attendant questions we have mentioned (such as alimony) at a later date, just as Patricia Vanderbilt did.

*Third:* Have your wife sign a Separation Settlement Agreement *before* you leave the home state. This should cover child custody, child support, alimony and property division. (See Chapter X on Separation Agreements.)

*Fourth:* Consult a lawyer in both states—your home state and the state to which you are moving. It's expensive, sure. But remember, it was *your* idea!

## F. Divorce in Another Country

First, let me say that there is absolutely no way to obtain a valid divorce in another country by mail order. Even if your wife appears "by mail" and you have a written property settlement, you cannot be divorced by a stand-in lawyer on foreign shores. Not in Mexico, or El Salvador or Nicaragua. Anywhere. So forget *that*.

If you were to physically appear in a foreign country for a divorce, your home state is not under the compulsion of the Constitution to recognize it. You would be going to needless trouble and expense with no guarantee of results. However, if you are an American citizen residing in a foreign country, the courts of the United States would be apt to recognize a divorce from your resident country.

All in all, there is nothing better—or safer—than a hometown divorce. But that doesn't keep you from checking into the feasibility of an out-of-state action if your road is rocky in your home state. This "checking into" gives you and your lawyer leverage when dealing with an obstinate about-to-be ex-wife. The thought that you just might leave the state or the country often brings out her more cooperative nature. Nevertheless, you want to obtain a divorce where it best suits your interests. Divorce is traumatic enough without having to spend the next several years *proving* its validity.

# CHAPTER IV

# Grounds: Telling It like
# It Really Wasn't

## A. Grounds: Fact and Fiction

Historically, civilizations have encouraged marriage; discouraged divorce. The laws on the books reflect these attitudes. In no other area of the law is there a greater disparity between what the law states and what the judges and lawyers do than in divorce cases. Why? Because thinking men know that it is unrealistic to try to keep a marriage alive that is already dead. Thinking men realize that as times change so do people's needs and so should their laws.

One of the most destructive holdovers from earlier times is the concept of *fault* in divorce. This is the doctrine that states that one party in the divorce is at fault and the other totally blameless. How absurd. In no human relationship can there be such a black-and-white judgment.

The waiting period is another law designed to defy and discourage divorce. Many states will employ the practice of requiring the marriage partners to wait a specified time between the filing and the time of the actual divorce. Designed as a "cooling off" period, it has more the affect of an "embittering period." When two adults have decided to end a marriage, forcing them to stay together often deepens the wounds and insures the bitterness.

A modern delaying tactic is to institute required conciliation services. New York, for example, practically compels its divorcing citizens to seek marriage counseling. The theory is noble. However, like so many state-financed services, it has a low batting average. A much more realistic and less costly approach is to have counseling services available for those who specifically seek and want them.

Gradually these laws requiring a show of fault are being modified to meet the changed times and modern needs. But old ideas persist and the laws they represent often change slowly. If you live in a state that has adopted the no-fault divorce law, you are indeed fortunate. For those of you who don't, let's look at the traditional "Grounds for Divorce."

## B. Traditional Fault "Grounds for Divorce"

### 1. *Adultery*

This favorite subject of novelists, playwrights and local gossips has traditionally been considered the most heinous violation of the marital vows. Until recently, England and sophisticated New York maintained adultery as the *only* ground for which a divorce could be obtained. In all states which have not adopted a complete no-fault concept of divorce, adultery still remains one of the grounds.

Adultery is generally defined as a voluntary act of sexual intercourse by a married person with a person other than the offender's husband or wife. Thus, the wife who is a victim of rape is not guilty of adultery. There are some amusing relics of sex prejudice in this area. Some states formerly held that for a man to be guilty of adultery, he had to be actually living on a more or less permanent basis in an adulterous relationship. But a single act of sexual intercourse on the part of the wife was sufficient to give the husband grounds for divorce.

While adultery is the most well-known of the grounds, it is relied upon only in a small porportion of cases. The reasons are obvious. People do not want to air dirty linen in public, nor damage their egos by recognizing their mates' infidelity. The welfare of the children is also a consideration. Most parents prefer that their children not know of the adulterous conduct of one of their parents. Frequently a husband guilty of adultery will give a more favorable property settlement to his wife if she agrees not to use adultery as a ground for the divorce and agrees not to tell the children about his conduct.

In addition to the debilitating aftereffects, adultery is hard to prove. It has often, if artlessly, been said that there are seldom eyewitnesses to adultery. For this reason, adultery may be proved by circumstantial evidence. A wife bearing a child not the husband's is good (though circumstantial) evidence of adultery.

## 2. *Desertion*

The precise definition of desertion varies from state to state. It is generally defined as the voluntary separation of one spouse from the other without justification and with intent to desert. Most states require that the desertion continue for a specific period of time before it can be a ground for divorce. This period varies between one and five years. Separation of one spouse from the other for the purpose of obtaining a divorce, is not desertion. Temporary absence from the home on business or other assignment, such as military service, does not constitute desertion.

Basically, desertion requires four elements:

1. Voluntary separation by one spouse from the other.
2. The intent not to resume marital cohabitation.
3. Separation without the consent of the other spouse.
4. Separation without justification.

Some states have held that when one party refuses to have sexual intercourse with the other, the refusal constitutes desertion. Other states have held that if the husband in good faith has provided reasonable living accommodations, refusal of the wife to live there constitutes desertion on the part of the wife. Obviously, if the parties consent to living apart, there is no desertion.

## 3. *Cruelty*

Cruelty is the ground for divorce most widely

relied upon in the United States. In any discussion of cruelty it becomes doubly clear that the law on the books and the law in action are quite different.

A famous English case which attempted to define cruelty was *Evans vs. Evans*, decided in 1790. The case illustrates how far we have come in practice, while maintaining the strict definition of cruelty in the law books. The essence of the definition of cruelty as laid down in the *Evans* case occurs when there is bodily harm or a reasonable apprehension of bodily harm. Injuries to the feelings are not sufficient, nor are "mere austerity of temper, petulance of manners, rudeness of language, a want of civil attention and accommodation, even occasional sallies of passion, if they do not threaten bodily harm. . . ." In other words, the husband could be mean as hell as long as he did not beat his wife.

To say the least, the *Evans* case presents a rather limited definition of cruelty. It seems to have arisen from the assumption that marital happiness is best secured by making marriage indissoluble. The reasoning goes that when the parties know that they are bound together for life, they will resolve their differences and make an effort to get along. If they are able to separate on less serious grounds, they will not make the effort and immorality will result.

We have come a long way from such notions. Experience teaches us that a far more serious type of cruelty is that inflicted upon the emotions, mind and spirit of the other.

A wide diversity of language is used to describe cruelty. Most state laws refer to extreme cruelty, while others refer to cruel and inhuman treatment.

Some states speak of indignity. Despite this diversity of definition, there is a tendency throughout the country to develop a general law of cruelty and a general definition of cruelty. In an uncontested divorce case the courts will often grant divorce on evidence of cruelty which would not qualify with the strict standards laid down in the law books. In many states an uncontested divorce on grounds of cruelty may almost be had for the asking. Testimony such as, "He swore at me," "He told me he didn't love me any more," is frequently given to establish cruelty in an uncontested divorce case. And the courts quietly grant the divorce.

Today the courts recognize that the purpose of making cruelty a ground for divorce is not to protect the plaintiff, but to enable the courts to dissolve marriages which have deteriorated so far that they no longer serve the interests of either the parties or society. Thus cruelty becomes almost a synonym for irreconcilable marital differences. Divorces can be granted without search for bodily symptoms or concern for precisely who is responsible.

There are infinite ways in which one person may inflict pain on another. Violence or threats of violence are cruelty. Unreasonable sexual demands may constitute cruelty. Refusal to have marital relations for a substantial period of time has been considered cruelty. Attacks on self-respect, insults in public, are considered cruelty. Neglect of the spouse, failure to support the wife and children, improper relations with persons of the opposite sex (short of adultery), all have been held to be cruelty.

Drunkenness and drug addiction have been

71

equated with cruelty, although sometimes these are listed as separate grounds for divorce.

General marital unkindness probably includes the great bulk of cruelty cases. The man who forces his wife to live with him in his mother's home has been held to be guilty of cruelty. The wife's insistence on having her mother live with her and her husband has been equated with cruelty.

Cruelty may consist of verbal abuse, name calling, nagging or refusing to speak at all. Cruelty can be threatening to harm the children or inducing the children to behave badly toward one of the spouses. Cruelty may be inflicted by a wife who is entirely preoccupied with her social life, drinks heavily, and wholly disregards the husband's desires for affection and comfort.

Active homosexual conduct on the part of one of the spouses has been held to be cruelty. In some cases there seems to be reason to argue that homosexual desires may not be within the defendant's control. In such a case it would seem wrong to hold a party legally responsible for conduct which he cannot avoid. But it would also be wrong to hold the other person in an untenable marriage situation.

Interestingly enough, the Women's Liberation Movement has given another dimension to this problem. I know of at least five cases where the wife has left her husband to live with another woman. I know of no legal case that specifically holds lesbian conduct to constitute cruelty; but presumably such conduct on the part of the wife would be considered cruelty. At least it should give the husband cause for divorce.

In a recent case, two males sued to force the authorities of the State of Minnesota to issue them a marriage license. They contended that preventing persons of the same sex from marrying is a violation of the equal protection of the laws provision of the Constitution. The court held against them. Heterosexual marriage is apparently still the only kind our society and its laws condone. There is one exception. Boulder County, Colorado, will issue marriage licenses to people of the same sex.

### 4. *Miscellaneous grounds*

Adultery, desertion and cruelty are grounds for divorce in all states that have not adopted a complete no-fault concept. Some states have established additional grounds such as nonsupport and neglect of duty. In these cases they must show that the husband was able to provide for his wife and family, but did not.

In some states, conviction for a felony is grounds for divorce by the other spouse.

In most states, incurable insanity is a ground. In such a case, fault is not a factor. Incurable insanity on the part of one spouse allows the other to obtain a divorce on that ground. However, most states specifically provide that the divorce does not relieve the one from supporting his incurably insane spouse. One difficulty in such cases is that few psychiatrists or psychologists are willing to testify that *anyone* is incurably insane.

Some states allow grounds for divorce which rightfully should be grounds for an annulment.

These include such grounds as a prior existing marriage, impotence, fraud, duress and incest.

The no-fault grounds of incompatibility, living separate and apart, and irreconcilable differences are discussed separately in this chapter.

## C. Traditional Defenses to Traditional Grounds

The defenses to the grounds for divorce developed in English ecclesiastical courts. These defenses are still on the books in many of our states. In practice they are rarely used, since by our standards they are archaic. Nevertheless, you should know that they exist because sometimes they are used.

### 1. *Connivance*

Connivance is the consent by one party to the other's misconduct. It is almost entirely limited to actions brought on grounds of adultery. Specifically, it applies if one party originally consented to the other's adultery. Connivance prevents the "consenting party" from withdrawing his consent and suing for divorce.

If one party actually participated in the other's adulterous conduct, connivance also applies. For example, a husband who exposes his wife to improper company and participates in the adultery by urging it be committed, is guilty of connivance. So is the husband who hires someone to seduce his wife. Believe it or not, such things have happened. I know of one case where the wife, wishing a divorce, hired a prostitute to secude her willing husband.

When the wife filed for divorce, charging adultery, the husband was able to show that his thoughtful wife had hired the prostitute. The wife's conduct constituted connivance and she was denied the divorce.

## 2. Collusion

Collusion is defined as an agreement between the husband and wife that one of them shall commit or appear to have committed acts constituting grounds for divorce for the purposes of enabling the other to obtain a divorce. The collusive act most relied upon is adultery. Collusion, too, originated as a defense to divorce in the English ecclesiastical courts and has become a part of American law. In about half of the states, collusion is recognized as a defense to divorce by statute; in many other states, it is a defense as a matter of general common law.

In certain respects, connivance and collusion are similar. The main distinction is that connivance depends upon the consent that the marital offense actually be committed, while collusion involves agreement that the marital offense only appear to have been committed.

## 3. Condonation

Condonation consists in condoning the marital offense committed by the other. Like connivance and collusion, it came into American law from the English ecclesiastical practice, and today it is governed by statute in about half of the states.

Some courts have even taken the position that condonation occurs when the parties resume sexual relations after one spouse learned of the other's wrong. Either resumption of sexual relations or forgiveness may constitute condonation.

There may be some justification for the doctrine of condonation. Even the trend to make divorce easier cannot argue with the policy of reconciliation whenever possible. If the parties can agree to forgive and forget the marital misconduct of either, then perhaps both can start afresh.

### 4. *Delay*

If a spouse has grounds for divorce but delays in bringing suit, he may not avail himself of the grounds later. As a practical matter, judges and lawyers give little credence to a party who complains of some ancient marital breach by his spouse.

I can recall several cases where a wife has come to me seeking a divorce on grounds of adultery. Upon close questioning, I found that the adultery occurred many years prior and that the parties had subsequently resumed normal marital relations. Clearly no court is going to go back in time and grant a divorce. The court will consider that the wife has forgiven the misconduct by her actions in resuming normal marital relations.

### 5. *Recrimination*

Recrimination, as I have previously stated, has been best defined as the outrageous legal principle which ordains that when both parties have grounds for a divorce, neither may have a divorce. Suppose a wife has grounds for divorce based on her husband's adultery. Suppose this husband can prove he has grounds based on his wife's cruelty. Application of the doctrine of recrimination would prevent either party from getting a divorce because both were at fault. Can you imagine a situation more ridiculous?

This doctrine prevents the dissolution of the marriage most appropriate for dissolution and insures that the quarreling spouses may never find happier marriages. It may be generally described as letting the parties "stew in their own juice." Marriage then becomes a form of punishment. Incredible as it may seem, the doctrine of recrimination is still embodied in the statutes of about half of our states.

In some states the courts may weigh the relative faults of the parties and still grant the divorce to either or both. This is called the doctrine of comparative rectitude. For instance, a husband may have committed adultery and his wife cruelty, the court can go ahead and grant the wife a divorce on the assumption that adultery is a more serious offense than cruelty. In some states the court can even grant both a divorce—to her for adultery, to him for cruelty.

## D. The Disadvantages of Fault Grounds

Any system that requires the placing of blame to obtain a divorce usually causes as many problems as it attempts to solve. Seeking fault augments the emotional trauma, increases the bitterness, encourages the name calling and heightens the recriminations.

Forcing both parties to recreate their private lives in court makes court proceedings a circus. Conducting these marital donnybrooks in the courts is a mockery of justice, an enormous expense to the parties and, indirectly, to the taxpayers. The fact should be that if the parties cannot get along, they should be divorced—quickly, cleanly, calmly, and hopefully with dignity.

## E. No-Fault Grounds for Divorce

Today the trend is to dissolve a failed marriage on the very grounds of its failure, not on the grounds of the fault of one or both of the parties—hence the term *No-Fault Divorce*. No-fault takes three forms—Incompatibility, Living Separate and Apart, and Irreconcilable Differences (sometimes called Irretrievable Marital Breakdown).

### 1. *Incompatibility*

Defined, incompatibility refers "to conflicts in personalities and dispositions so deep as to be irreconcilable and to render it impossible for the parties to continue a normal marital relationship with each other." In other words, when a marriage has failed, the court should dissolve it. Incompatibility as a ground for divorce exists in Alaska, New Mexico, Guam and the Virgin Islands.

None of these incompatibility statutes mention fault. But the courts are so ingrained with it that they have frequently held that incompatibility must be shown on the part of the defendant. Oh, how the old ideas linger on!

## 2. *Living separate and apart*

Living separate and apart is now recognized as a ground for divorce in about half of the states. Without finding fault on the part of either party, the court recognizes that the marriage has failed. Statutes in the various states determine the necessary length of the separation before a divorce can be granted. However, if the parties resume living together, the separation no longer constitutes grounds for divorce.

The states that provide living separate and apart as a ground for divorce fall into three categories:

1. Those states that require the husband and wife to obtain a Judgment of Separation *before* they separate. They must then remain apart pursuant to the Separation Judgment a specified length of time before applying for divorce.

2. Those states that require the parties to voluntarily or willingly live apart for the necessary period of time.

3. Those states whose statutes allow the divorce upon proof that the parties have lived apart for the necessary period of time, without considering the question of the willingness of either to the separation.

## 3. *Irreconcilable differences and irretrievable marital breakdown*

Seven states now have abolished all the grounds

previously mentioned and simply provide irreconcil-able differences, irretrievable marital breakdown, or simply marital breakdown as the sole ground for divorce. Regardless of the name given, the meaning is the same.

Irreconcilable differences and irretrievable mari-tal breakdown are defined as those differences which have caused the irremediable breakdown of the marriage. In other words, if the court determines that there are substantial reasons for not continuing the marriage, the marriage should be dissolved. As California is such a state, I simply have my client testify that there are irreconcilable differences, that the marriage has irreparably broken down and that it should be dissolved.

## F. Advantages of No-Fault Divorce

One of the obvious advantages of no-fault divorce is that it lessens the personal trauma and bitterness. This is not to say that the people going through such a divorce are not emotionally upset. They are. But they are relieved of the burden of recrimination and name calling. They are no longer forced to justify their conduct. Relieved of such burdens, the emotional upsets are far easier to bear.

A second advantage is that it makes settlements easier. No longer forced to point fingers, the parties are much more inclined to sit down and dispas-sionately settle the questions of custody, visitation, child support, alimony and property division.

Thanks to No-Fault, affairs, peccadilloes, and casual encounters are not admissible evidence in court. The past remains in the past. What you did or why you did it matters not at all.

The grounds for divorce in the various states are listed in Appendix A. Consult this appendix, but by all means consult your lawyer too. Don't listen to the wisdom of the fellow in the local pub or the guy in the next chair at the barber shop.

The state legislatures are changing our divorce laws with every session. You may be that fellow whose wife has been telling him, "I'll never give you a divorce!" If your state has adopted No-Fault, the divorce is not hers to give. It's yours for the asking!

# CHAPTER V

# Procedures: Unmasking the Hocus-Pocus

A divorce is an emotional experience, and when you have emotion, you have confusion. Too often lawyers do not take the time to explain the details of divorce proceedings to their emotional and confused clients. The result is that, as the divorce proceeds, the client becomes *more* confused. Let me try to bring a little light to the dark corners of divorce procedure.

To the nonlawyer, there is a certain mystique to the law. Legal procedure the client often views as little more than a ritual of hocus-pocus that is designed to confuse, delay, and make it appear that the lawyer is doing a heck of a lot of work so he can charge a big bill.

Actually, the rules and procedures have been worked out over a long period of time. They are intended to achieve desirable social goals, and to a large extent they succeed. Let's talk about these procedures which, after all, are intended for your protection.

## A. Starting the Divorce

When I started to practice law, it was thought that the gentlemanly thing to do was to let the wife file for divorce. Vestigial chivalry allowed the husband to be the "bad guy." Today, people are more aware of the realities of life. A man as well as a woman may wish to end the miserable union. Either should feel free to go to the lawyer and have him prepare the necessary documents.

## B. The Complaint (or Petition) and Summons

The first document that is prepared is known as the Complaint for Divorce. In some states it is called a Petition, in others, a Bill of Divorce. Basically, this document sets forth the essential facts of the marriage and requests that the court grant a divorce to the party who filed. The facts of the marriage include:

1. The names of the parties.
2. When and how long they were married.
3. The number and ages of the children.
4. When the parties separated.
5. The extent of the property.
6. The needs of the parties.
7. Grounds (see Chapter IV). Usually grounds are stated in general terms. Extreme cruelty, as we have noted, is the ground most generally relied upon.

At the time the lawyer prepares the Complaint, he usually prepares the Summons. When the lawyer files the Complaint, the court clerk signs the original Summons. This is called "issuing" the Summons. A copy of the Complaint together with a copy of the Summons is served upon the other party by a sheriff, marshal or other authorized person. In addition to personal service, service may be obtained upon the other party by publication in a local newspaper. Service other than personal is provided for in the statutes of the various states. However, personal service upon the other party is the method most commonly employed.

The Summons, having been issued by the clerk of the court, directs the other party to appear in person, through an attorney, and to file a written answer to the Complaint within a specified time.

In the event that the party served does not answer or respond within the allowed time, the party who filed the Complaint may obtain the divorce by default in most states.

## C. The Answer (or Response) and Cross-Complaint

Let us assume your wife has filed first and you have been served. You and your lawyer read all the allegations in her Complaint and either admit or deny them. Your written Answer is called simply the Answer; in some states, the Response.

If you live in a state where fault grounds are used, you will admit or deny whatever she charges. You will challenge the proposed property division, custody, visitation—whatever she proposes that you think is unfair.

In states where one of the fault grounds must be alleged, you may wish to cross-complain for divorce yourself. In your cross-complaint you allege that you too have grounds for divorce and set forth your allegations in the same way she did. The cross-complaint is similar to the divorce complaint, and in it you must state (allege) all the essential facts contained in the complaint.

## D. Temporary Orders

Since the husband is most often the breadwinner, it is the husband who usually has control of the money. Were he to leave home he could starve out the wife and children by refusing to give them money. This brutish tactic is frequently adopted by the husband who is seeking vengeance. It is also a ploy of the husband who is trying to obtain a favorable property division. I heartily condemn such conduct. Not only is it unfair, but it puts the man in a very bad light with the court.

To avoid this "starving out" tactic, the law has devised a system called "temporary orders," which provide for custody, child support, alimony, visitation, and other living arrangements on a temporary basis. Another purpose of the temporary order is to preserve the status quo. It may prevent either party from hiding assets or grabbing the children and running out of the state.

Assuming that your wife has filed a Complaint for Divorce and she and her lawyer feel that you may not voluntarily make alimony and child-support payments, her lawyer will prepare a document which is called an Order to Show Cause. This is signed by the judge. The Order to Show Cause is then served upon you. It orders you to show cause why certain specified temporary orders should not be made.

Her lawyer will also have prepared an affidavit which sets forth the reasons for the amount of support your wife is requesting.

Another way to obtain temporary orders is for her lawyer to prepare and file a Motion requesting the court to make the temporary orders. These devices serve the same purpose, whether called an Order to Show Cause or a Motion. Both protect the wife and children and seek to preserve the status quo.

The Order to Show Cause or Motion for temporary orders is usually made at the beginning of the divorce action and is frequently filed simultaneously with the Complaint for Divorce.

The Order to Show Cause or Motion sets a hearing date in court. At the hearing the lawyers for both parties present their evidence. The wife's lawyer will attempt to show her needs and the husband's ability to meet those needs. The husband's lawyer will often attempt to show that the husband does not have the ability to meet the wife's demands as she has stated them. The judge then decides how much the wife shall be paid and a temporary order is made.

As already mentioned, temporary orders may also include provisions for child custody, child visitation, and child support. They may direct the husband to pay the wife a specific amount of money each month for child support. Again, the amount is based upon the needs of the children and the ability of the husband to pay. In making orders for child support, the court considers the resources of the wife. If she works or if she has other means, she may be ordered to contribute toward child support.

Temporary orders frequently spell out the living arrangements. The wife and children are generally allowed to live in the family home while the husband is ordered to move out. Such orders also enjoin the parties from hiding the assets of the marriage and from harassing each other.

Temporary orders usually include provisions for attorneys' fees. If the wife has no resources she obviously cannot afford to pay a lawyer. Accordingly, the court will order the husband to pay her attorney's fees and court costs on account.

Sometimes the parties think that after they have been to court for the temporary orders they are divorced. They are not. Don't confuse a court hearing on temporary orders with the divorce trial itself.

## E. Discovery Proceedings

Let us assume that the Complaint for Divorce has been filed by your wife, you have been served, and you have filed an answer through your lawyer. Let us further assume that temporary orders have been made providing for child support, alimony, custody and visitation arrangements, her attorney's fees and court costs. Both of you have been restrained from hiding assets and from annoying each other.

What happens next? It is at this point that your attorney and hers undertake what is called "discovery." What are they seeking to discover?

*First:* Each lawyer wants to find out what evidence the other side intends to use as grounds for divorce.

*Second:* Each lawyer wants to find out the full extent and value of the property.

*Third:* Each lawyer wants to find out the full extent of the income and potential income of both parties.

*Fourth:* If custody is an issue, each lawyer wants to discover facts that would determine which party should have custody.

## 1. *Written interrogatories*

Written interrogatories are questions prepared by the attorney for one party which the other party must answer under oath and in writing. Your attorney may direct written interrogatories to your wife; her attorney may do the same to you. The written interrogatories procedure is the least expensive method of discovery.

## 2. *Depositions*

Instead of questions in writing, the deposition is an oral examination of one of the parties. Depositions are usually taken in the lawyer's office. The party whose deposition is being taken (called the deponent) is questioned by the other's attorney. He or she is under oath. The questions and answers are taken down by a court reporter and later typed into booklet form.

The deponent has the opportunity to read his deposition and make corrections to his answers. He is then asked to sign the deposition. The signature is not mandatory because an unsigned deposition may still be used in court.

Before your deposition is taken, your lawyer will prepare you in advance by asking you the questions he anticipates her attorney will ask. Your attorney will be present and will not let you be trapped or taken advantage of. Although the deposition is somewhat of an informal proceeding, remember, it is just as if you were on the witness stand answering questions in court.

### 3. *Appraisals and financial reports*

When the value of marital property is in dispute, appraisals of the property become necessary. If the value of a business is being disputed, the financial records of the business and the reports of certified public accountants are important. There are accountants who specialize in making appraisals of businesses as well as of medical, dental, veterinarian, engineering and legal practices.

Each party has a right to have these appraisals and all the financial reports and accountings. The purpose is to establish the value of the property, tangible and intangible, so there can be a fair division of the total assets of the marriage.

### F. Settling Out of Court

Over 90 per cent of divorce cases are settled without a trial. By the time discovery is completed, each party has a good idea of the strengths and weaknesses of his case and the strengths and weaknesses of the other's case, the value of the property, the income of each party, and what the court is likely to decide.

It is at this point that the true art of the lawyer becomes important. One of the main jobs of the lawyer is to second-guess what a judge will do. By second-guessing what the court will do, your lawyer can achieve the same results for you without having to go to the expense, time and emotional stress of a trial. A written separation agreement which settles all the issues of the divorce is then prepared and signed by both of you. (See Chapter X on Separation Agreement.) If your lawyer can negotiate a favorble settlement that is fair to you and your wife, you will have achieved great success (if it can be said that anyone achieves success in a divorce).

If, however, you or your wife feel that the other's demands are unfair—and you refuse to sign—it becomes necessary to take the divorce to court to decide in a trial.


## G. Waiting for the Trial

Courts are crowded and you must wait your turn. After all the necessary papers (pleadings) have been filed, after discovery has been completed, after appraisals and accountings are finished, either your lawyer or hers will file a memorandum asking the court to set a trial date. How soon you will get to trial before a judge depends, of course, on how many cases are ahead of you. Sometimes it will take a month, sometimes it will take a year or more. Waiting is debilitating. Try to settle out of court.

## H. The Trial

The trial is almost always before a judge. A jury is rarely used in a divorce proceeding. The reasons are historical and practical. In the old English ecclesiastical courts juries were nonexistent in divorce proceedings; therefore no precedent was set. The practical reason for not using the jury is that the issues involved in divorce litigation are complex. It is not an issue of guilt or innocence, liability or nonliability, or determining an award of damages. Divorce litigation involves a multitude of issues: the welfare of children; their custody; the parties' rights of visitation to the children; the question of child support, which is of course dependent upon the many factors we have discussed; alimony, which is also dependent upon many factors; the division of property, which in turn is dependent upon the evaluation of the property. The issues are far too complex for a jury to handle with any degree of efficiency. The judge has usually heard a lot of divorce cases and has had years of experience in listening to similar problems.

It is at the trial that you must prove what you have said in your pleadings. If it is necessary to prove the fault of the other party, it is at the trial that you must prove it. If it is necessary to prove that you should have custody of the children, if it is necessary to prove need for specific visitation rights, it is at trial that you must prove your contentions. If child support and alimony are at issue, it is at trial you must prove your true ability to pay and your wife's and children's true needs. It is at the trial that you must prove why you should be awarded what you request.

### 1. Courtroom etiquette

Despite what you may see on television and in movies, the experienced trial lawyer is extremely courteous, not only to the judge but to the opposing attorney, the opposing party and the witnesses for the opposing party. In addition to courtesy for its own sake, the trial lawyer's courtesy is based on practicability and precedent. A court of law is the home of justice. When you honor the judge, you show respect for all mankind.

Therefore, in court, take your cue from your lawyer. Never lose your temper, no matter how provoked; never shout; never appear to be vindictive or express a desire to be anything but fair. Your manly demeanor can be your most influential witness. Remember, the judge is judging you. He will have great respect for your courtesy and reasonableness.

### 2. Courtroom tactics

Courtroom tactics are not tricks. Your case is not going to be won—or lost—by some magican maneuver of your lawyer. But your case can be helped—or harmed—by how you appear on the witness stand. So here are the primary rules:

*Tactic 1:* Courtesy, as we have just discussed, is your primary tactic.

*Tactic 2:* Calmness. Your wife's lawyer is going to try hard to make you lose your temper, to make you say things you will regret, to make you boast about the extent of your property, your job and your income. He will try to find discrepancies in your testimony. Some may call discrepancies lies, but never use that word. Your calm demeanor will add strength to your testimony. Take your time in answering his barbs. It's easy to lash out when you feel cornered, hard to remain calm. So take a deep breath to steady your nerves.

*Tactic 3:* Courage. You will be advised by your lawyer always to be truthful, even when your answers are distasteful, humiliating or damaging to your case. I remember observing a paternity case in court. The man alleged to be the father was on the stand. When asked if it were possible that the child could be his, he very honestly answered that, yes, it was possible. The honesty of his answer so impressed the judge that he found in the man's favor on the point at issue. Think of the humiliating situation this man was placed in and how one simple honest answer saved the day for him.

*Tactic 4:* Conciseness. The best witness answers questions directly and with as *few words as possible.* A simple "yes" or "no" or "I don't know" or "I don't remember" will usually suffice. The temptation on the stand is to list all your grievances against your wife. Resist it. Answer the questions, but be brief!

You can't expect a judge to listen to twenty or

thirty years of your complaints against your wife. The courtroom is not a psychiatrist's couch. But more important than boring the judge is the damage you might inflict upon yourself. I recall the case of one particularly experienced trial lawyer who was brilliant at cross-examination. He was a handsome man who thought he had quite a way with the ladies. In this particular case he represented the husband, who was trying to prove that his wife had been unfaithful. When it came time to cross-examine the wife he approached the witness box in gleeful anticipation, a wry smile on his lips. First he was charming, cooing his questions as if he were sitting across from her in an expensive restaurant. She answered with a brief yes—or no. Next he became menacing, threatening. Still she remained unruffled—and unwordy. Next he came on with the big-brother you-can-tell-me-everything approach. All he got was yes—or no. After five hours of cross-examining, Mr. Smooth gave up. The wife had been well prepared. Her calm, courageous demeanor in face of this onslaught won her case for her.

## 3. *The judge's job*

Pity the poor judge in the divorce trial. Whatever decision he makes, both parties are usually going to be unhappy. It is he who must decide custody. It is he who must decide the visitation privileges of the noncustodial parent. It is he who must decide the extent of child support. It is he who must try to find the money for two households when there is barely enough for one. The judge is asked to have the wisdom of Solomon, the patience of Job, the scholarship of Holmes, the compassion of St. Francis and the insight of Freud. His decisions weigh heavily upon him. Your courtesy and courtroom etiquette will lighten his load and most certainly aid your cause.

# CHAPTER VI

# Alimony: Paying for
# a Dead Horse

## A. What It Is

Alimony. The very word conjures up visions of the gay divorcee living in a penthouse while her "ex" slaves away at three jobs to support her lifestyle; of showgirls soaking the old boys after six months of marriage; of grasping harpies and broken men. To men, few words can evoke such blind emotional hatred, aversion and distaste.

These emotions and visions are, with a few notable exceptions, becoming fainter. Fear not. From a monetary standpoint, alimony has had to become more realistic. Most men cannot afford to support two households in the same style in which they supported one. The courts are well aware of this.

Alimony may be defined as payment by one spouse to the other for the support of the spouse paid. In the vast majority of cases it is the husband who pays his ex-wife alimony. It is founded on the theory that the husband has an obligation to support his wife or ex-wife; if not wholly, then partially. Furthermore, it is an obligation that is *not* dischargeable in bankruptcy.

The custom of awarding alimony originated, like many of our divorce laws, in the English ecclesiastical courts. You will recall that these courts did not give a complete divorce, but merely authorized husband and wife to live separate and apart. Therefore, ordering the husband to pay his wife alimony simply recognized his continuing obligation to support his wife. In those days a married woman could not own property. Even the property a woman possessed before marriage came under her husband's control after marriage. She could not enter into her own business, and employment opportunities were negligible. Consequently, alimony served an important social purpose *then*.

Today, however, divorce is complete and the parties are free to remarry. Each receives a share of the marital property. Women have employment opportunities that were unheard of a hundred years ago. Therefore, under modern conditions there is little logical justification for alimony.

I think every divorced man secretly (sometimes not so secretly) resents paying alimony. Most men feel that the end of a marriage should be the end of his obligations to his wife. In most cases alimony represents a hardship on the man and a strain on any subsequent marriage.

I have known men to be so emotionally opposed to paying alimony that they give away much more property than they should have simply to avoid the alimony obligation. This is not just perverseness on the part of men. There is a logic involved that says a woman who does not want to be married to a man has no right to expect that man to support her.

The legislature and courts, however, still tend to the ancient view that maintains that the ex-wife deserves support, if only partial, as her right from the dissolved marriage. She did invest time and effort (theoretically) in the man and he should repay her investment.

## B. The Forms Alimony May Take

Alimony is generally paid by the husband to the wife in periodic, usually monthly, installments. Alimony terminates upon the wife's death or remarriage. It may also terminate upon the order of a court, the happening of certain other events, or after a specified time.

Alimony may also take the form of a lump sum payable all at once or in installments. Lump-sum alimony does have the advantage of certainty. Both parties can make plans with the knowledge that the sum is fixed, that it will be neither increased nor decreased.

You should bear in mind that alimony is payment for your wife's needed support. It is not payment by way of a property division. There are important tax consequences to this distinction that we shall discuss later.

## C. What Alimony Is Based Upon

Alimony is based upon several things. First, the wife's needs. If your wife works and is earning a good living, her needs from you will be less. In such cases the courts frequently will not award her alimony. If your wife has independent means, such as an inheritance, courts would be loath to award her alimony. On the other hand, if your wife does not work, has not worked in a long time, or has few skills and little potential for obtaining employment, you can expect that the court will award her alimony.

The second criterion for awarding alimony is the husband's ability to pay. Your ability at least sets the outside limits to your obligation. If you earn a great deal or have tremendous resources, the courts are inclined to be more generous in awarding alimony. Your earnings and resources are also reflected in the lifestyle to which you accustomed your wife. Many courts have said that it is the husband's obligation to support his wife in the style in which he accustomed her to live. This is very pleasant for her, if he can afford it. The lifestyle approach seems to be best applied in cases of the wealthy.

A third factor the courts consider in awarding alimony is the length of the marriage. If your marriage is of long duration and your wife has not worked for some time, her employment potential is limited. The courts will consider these factors in awarding alimony. Suppose you have been married thirty-one years, your wife is fifty-three and hasn't worked in the past twenty-five years. She has stayed in the home and reared the children. As a result she has lost her job skills. Unless the property settlement is large enough for her to live upon the income from her share, the court is apt to be generous in awarding her alimony. Certainly the court is not going to leave her destitute.

On the other hand, if your marriage is of short duration, it is presumed your wife can re-enter the job market. In such cases, the court would probably award alimony for a limited period of time covering her adjustment to her new life. This would be the case of a man married for five years, whose wife was a top-flight secretary. If her health is good, she can find employment quickly. The court would most likely award alimony for enough time for her to find a job. But, you say, what if she doesn't go out and aggressively seek a job? How long is "time to find employment"? Courts will determine a reasonable length of time. They won't let her take forever.

A fourth aspect of alimony is punitive. Historically, courts have considered the degree of fault of the husband in awarding alimony to the wife. If the husband were greatly at fault, the court would award more alimony than if his transgressions were minor. Under this concept, alimony is in the nature of damages paid by the husband to the wife for his wrongdoing. Similarly, if the wife had misconducted herself, the courts did not award her alimony. It is this punitive aspect that gives alimony stigma and causes further resentment on the part of the husband. Fortunately, this punitive, or damage, aspect is lessening. Today most courts consider alimony for what it should be—a contribution by the husband for the needy wife's support.

In those enlightened states which have abolished fault as a ground for divorce, the term *alimony* has been eliminated and the term *spousal support* substituted. The concept of alimony as punishment to the party that transgressed the marriage is eliminated. Thus both the stigma and the word are removed.

### D. The Income Tax Aspects of Alimony

Alimony may be deductible by the husband from his federal income tax. Conversely, it is then *taxable* to the wife.

Sometimes husbands like to pay their wives a lump sum as alimony and have it over with, or fix a lump sum and pay in monthly installments. This arrangement has tax dangers for the husband. Uncle Sam may consider this arrangement a division of property, in which case it would not be deductible by the husband nor taxable to the wife.

It is important for you to remember that *installment* payments on a fixed lump sum are deductible to you *only* if:

1. the installments exceed a ten-year period;
2. not more than 10 per cent of the lump sum is paid in any one year;
3. the obligation to pay the lump sum will in any event terminate upon the death or remarriage of the wife.

Since the rules of the Internal Revenue Service are constantly changing, you should thoroughly discuss the tax aspects of alimony with your attorney.

## E. Turning Alimony to Your Advantage

It is possible to calculate your alimony payment so that Uncle Sam will be paying a large part of it. Separation agreements are frequently drawn so that alimony is based on a sliding scale related to the husband's increase or decrease in income. The more the husband earns, the more alimony he will pay. A good part of what the husband is paying would be taken away from him in income taxes anyhow. Why not pay it to the wife rather than the IRS? Consider a few examples:

1. Henry Thomas has a net taxable income after his personal exemption and all deductions of $15,000 a year.

    a. Assume he pays no alimony:

| | |
|---|---:|
| Taxable income | $ 15,000 |
| Federal income tax (approx.) | 3,520 |
| Net income | $ 11,480 |

    b. Next, assume Mr. Thomas pays $200 per month in alimony:

| | |
|---|---:|
| Taxable income after alimony | $ 12,600 |
| Federal tax | 2,804 |
| Net income after alimony and tax | $ 9,796 |
| | |
| Tax without alimony | $ 3,520 |
| Tax with alimony | 2,804 |
| Saved | $ 716 |

He will have paid $1,684 out of pocket in alimony and Uncle Sam will have paid $716 of his alimony.

    c. Next, assume Mr. Thomas pays $300 per month alimony:

| | |
|---|---:|
| Taxable income after alimony | $ 11,400 |
| Federal tax | 2,468 |
| Net income after alimony and tax | $ 8,932 |

| Tax without alimony | $ 3,520 |
| Tax with alimony | 2,468 |
| Saved | $ 1,052 |

He will have paid $2,548 out of pocket in alimony. Uncle Sam will have paid $1,052 of his alimony.

d. Next, assume Mr. Thomas pays $400 per month alimony:

| Taxable income after alimony | $ 10,200 |
| Federal tax | 2,144 |
| Net income after alimony and tax | $ 8,056 |

| Tax without alimony | $ 3,520 |
| Tax with alimony | 2;144 |
| Saved | $ 1,376 |

He will have paid $3,424 out of pocket in alimony. Uncle Sam will have paid $1,376 of his alimony.

2. Peter Smith has a net taxable income after deductions of $25,000 a year.

a. Assume he pays no alimony:

| Taxable income | $ 25,000 |
| Federal tax | 7,190 |
| Net income | $ 17,810 |

b. Next, assume he pays $500 per month alimony:

| Taxable income after alimony | $ 19,000 |
| Federal tax | 4,870 |
| Net income after alimony and tax | $ 14,130 |

| Tax without alimony | $ 7,190 |
| Tax with alimony | 4,870 |
| Saved | $ 2,320 |

He pays $3,680 out of pocket alimony. Uncle Sam pays $2,320 of his alimony.

103

c. Next, assume he pays $800 per month alimony:

| | |
|---|---:|
| Taxable income after alimony | $ 15,400 |
| Federal tax | 3,644 |
| Net income after alimony and tax | $ 11,756 |

| | |
|---|---:|
| Tax without alimony | $ 7,190 |
| Tax with alimony | 3,644 |
| Saved | $ 3,546 |

He pays $6,054 out of pocket in alimony. Uncle Sam pays $3,546 of his alimony.

3. John Adams has an income from all sources, after deductions, of $50,000 yearly.

a. Assume he pays no alimony:

| | |
|---|---:|
| Taxable income | $ 50,000 |
| Federal tax | 20,190 |
| Net income | $ 29,810 |

b. Next, assume he pays $1,000 per month alimony:

| | |
|---|---:|
| Taxable income after alimony | $ 38,000 |
| Federal tax | 13,290 |
| Net income after alimony and tax | $ 24,710 |

| | |
|---|---:|
| Tax without alimony | $ 20,190 |
| Tax with alimony | 13,210 |
| Saved | $ 6,980 |

He will have paid out of pocket alimony of $5,020. Uncle Sam will pay $6,980 of his alimony. At this point Uncle Sam is paying more than he does in alimony.

c. Next, assume he pays $2,000 per month alimony:

| | |
|---|---:|
| Taxable income after alimony | $ 26,000 |
| Federal tax after alimony | 7,590 |
| Net income after alimony and tax | $ 18,410 |

104

| Tax without alimony | $ 20,190 |
| Tax with alimony | 7,590 |
| Saved | $ 12,600 |

He will pay $11,400 out of pocket in alimony. Uncle Sam will pay $12,600 of his alimony.

4. Aaron Hamilton has an income from all sources, after deductions, of $100,000 yearly.

a. Assume he pays no alimony:

| Taxable income | $100,000 |
| Federal tax | 53,000 |
| Net income | $ 47,000 |

b. Assume he pays $1,000 per month alimony:

| Taxable income after alimony | $ 88,000 |
| Federal tax | 44,830 |
| Net income after alimony and tax | $ 43,170 |

| Tax without alimony | $ 53,000 |
| Tax after paying alimony | 44,830 |
| Saved | $ 8,170 |

He pays only $3,830 in alimony. Uncle Sam pays $8,170 of his alimony.

c. Assume he pays $2,000 per month alimony:

| Taxable income after alimony | $ 76,000 |
| Federal tax | 36,750 |
| Net income after alimony and tax | $ 39,250 |

| Tax without paying alimony | $ 53,000 |
| Tax after paying alimony | 36,750 |
| Saved | $ 16,250 |

He pays only $7,750 out of pocket in alimony. Uncle Sam pays a whopping $16,250 of his alimony.

These figures do not take into account state income taxes, which most states have. There is also a savings in state income taxes. The obvious principle to deduce from these examples is that the higher one's income and the more alimony one pays, the greater is the proportion of the alimony that is paid by the federal government.

If you are in a high income tax bracket, it would be to your advantage to pay a high alimony in consideration for your wife, allowing you to keep a greater proportion of the property. By all means, this is an area that you want to go over very carefully with your lawyer.

## F. Reducing (and Increasing) Alimony

What if something happens and you can no longer afford to pay your ex-wife the alimony ordered or agreed to be paid? Is it possible to get alimony reduced? Yes. The basis for reducing alimony is "change of circumstances," either yours or hers.

What are the changes in circumstances that the courts consider sufficient to warrant a reduction in alimony? A change in her circumstances could be that she has advanced in her occupation and is making substantially more money. If she has come into an inheritance, this is also a change.

Similarly, a change in your circumstances for the worse can be the basis for reducing alimony. If you have lost your job, or suffered business reverses, you certainly have endured a change of circumstances. Just be sure that any business reverses are honest and not a bookkeeping scheme to show that the business is off. Your wife's attorney will investigate. If he can prove that your business reverses are not true reverses, you will not get your reduction. On top of that you will have incurred expenses, in attorney's fees and court costs.

Certain changes of circumstances are not considered sufficient for obtaining a reduction in alimony. For example, if you remarry, the courts generally do not consider this a change of circumstances. The theory is that you already had the obligation to your previous wife when you entered into the second marriage. Frequently the second wife will have to go to work to help pay alimony to the first wife. Needless to say, that result is a most undesirable situation which sometimes undermines the chances of success for the second marriage.

Courts take a jaundiced view of the man who quits his job and then asks to have his alimony reduced. In such cases the courts will consider that the man has the potential to earn at least as much as he was earning in his old job and will refuse to reduce alimony.

Remember, too, that the "ex" can also ask the court to increase her alimony based upon a change of circumstances. If she has become ill, unable to work, and you can afford to pay more, that would be considered a change of circumstances. Generally, if the needs become greater and your ability to pay increases, you run the danger that a court will increase the alimony.

Frequently in a divorce judgment the wife is awarded one dollar a year alimony, or the question of alimony is specifically reserved. This means that if the ex-wife later needs alimony, she can come into court and ask that it be increased. However, in most states once she has waived alimony, she can never again come into court and ask for it.

If the husband strikes it rich, does the ex-wife have a right to share in his new-found fortune? The answer is no. In one famous case, the wife got a divorce while the husband was making $7,500 per year. He was ordered to pay $75 per month alimony. Years later, an invention of his made him a millionaire. His wife went into court and asked for her alimony to be increased commensurate with his new lifestyle. The court held that she was entitled only to be supported on the scale which she enjoyed at the time of the divorce. She could not be granted an increase in alimony based solely on the husband's new wealth. The purpose of alimony is to care for the ex-wife's needs, not to provide her with a lifetime profit-sharing plan. A most salutary decision.

Suppose you think you have valid reasons for reducing your alimony. What do you do? First you consult your lawyer, who prepares the necessary papers and files them in court, asking the court to modify the divorce judgment to reduce the alimony. You will be asked to sign various affidavits, setting forth the reasons for the requested reduction. Sometimes the wife and the wife's attorney will agree that your grounds are valid, and will agree to the reduction. More often there will be a hearing in court. The question will be whether there has been a sufficient change in circumstances to entitle you to the reduction. It is up to you to prove the change of circumstances. You and your lawyer must be prepared with pay records, books of account and the canceled checks to show that you have genuinely had business reverses, lost your job or had a reduction in income.

If you are claiming a reduction based on your ex-wife's change of circumstances, you must be able to show her greater income, inheritance, or what-have-you. Don't rely on hearsay or little tales the children tell you. You have to be able to *prove* your point.

## G. Terminating Alimony

Frequently the divorce judgment or the separation agreement provides that alimony shall terminate on a specific date. When the date arrives the alimony obligation ceases.

Death of the wife obviously terminates alimony. Whether alimony terminates upon the husband's death varies from state to state. In most states alimony terminates upon the husband's death; in others it terminates unless the parties have agreed otherwise in the separation agreement.

The remarriage of the ex-wife will terminate your obligation to pay alimony. In some states this happens automatically, but in others you must apply to the court for an order terminating alimony. Here again, you should consult a lawyer as to the law of your state.

Suppose the ex-wife's second marriage doesn't work out and she gets an annulment. Does your alimony obligation revive? In some states it does. In most states it does not, for the very good reason that you should not be made the underwriter of your former wife's subsequent marital disasters.

Suppose your wife does not remarry, but starts living with another man. As long as this liaison is of short duration, the courts will usually not terminate alimony. This situation exemplifies an amusing inconsistency in the way our courts operate. Frequently the courts take a high moral tone in awarding the wife alimony at the beginning. After the divorce, when her subsequent indiscretions are revealed, the courts will generally say that she owes her former husband no particular obligation to remain chaste; that her immorality is not adultery, and what she does should be of no more concern to him than to any other member of society.

If, however, your ex-wife continues to live with a man for some length of time and it appears that she is being supported by him, you can ask the court to terminate or at least reduce alimony. The basis would be a change of circumstances. Certainly you should not be asked to support her friend!

Some states now provide that if the wife continues to live with a man on a more or less permanent basis, or holds herself out as married to her inamorato, these situations constitute sufficient grounds for termination of alimony.


## H. New Attitudes Toward Alimony

Today, alimony is largely an anachronism. Women can now own property, go into business and enjoy nearly equal employment opportunities. Their economic horizons are constantly expanding. Consequently, various state legislatures tend to discourage or to limit alimony. The courts have followed this legislative lead by sharply limiting the period a husband is required to pay alimony. The exception is the wife who clearly has little ability to support herself and needs alimony to exist.

The Women's Liberation Movement has contributed substantially to the decline of alimony. Equal pay for equal work strikes us as fundamentally fair. As the goals and objectives of Women's Liberation are realized, we may expect that alimony, except in rare cases, will become a thing of the past. (I wonder if the girls thought about that.)

## I. Alimony for Men

Originally, alimony was awarded only to the ex-wife. Today most American states provide that alimony may be awarded to men. It's still a rarity, but one can imagine a case of an invalid man seeking help from his working wife. Should she not be expected to support her former husband?

While legally men may have a right to alimony, don't count on it. The concept of chivalry still hangs heavy in the courts.

## J. What Happens When the Husband Doesn't Pay

Suppose you've been ordered to pay alimony to your ex-wife and you don't pay it. You can be hauled into court for contempt. In this procedure your wife must show:

(1) that you knew that you were obligated to pay alimony;

(2) that you have the ability to pay the alimony;

(3) that you willfully failed to pay the alimony.

If she can prove all these conditions, the court will order you to pay or go to jail. The important fact to remember is that the court *must* find that you do have the ability to pay. To avoid contempt you must show that you were unable to pay, not that the payment was inconvenient or difficult to make. My advice is always to pay something to show good faith. You can make up the arrearage later.

Contempt is not the only process for enforcing alimony awards. Your wife, through her lawyer, may execute on your assets, including bank accounts, brokerage accounts, real property. She may even have your wages garnished. As a young eager attorney just starting practice, I represented the wife of an older, socially prominent attorney. He was a colorful figure in the community who thought he was above the law and didn't pay his alimony. Rather than take him into court and furnish him with an arena for his antics, I simply let the arrearages accumulate. When they reached a goodly sum I quietly executed on his law partnership bank account. Within a few days the prestigious firm's checks went merrily bouncing all over town. When the reason was discovered, I received a frantic phone call from one of the partners saying they would send a certified check by special messenger if I would *please* release the account. Forever after, my satisfied client received her checks on time.

The order for assignment of wages is another diabolical device for collecting alimony. Your ex-wife can get a court order directing you to have your employer pay her directly from your wages. She can also get a charging order with the same result if you are in business as a partner. She can even get a receiver appointed to manage your business or other assets and collect the arrearage. These procedures can be embarrassing, even detrimental to your business. Keep this in mind when you contemplate letting your alimony payments lag.

## K. Enforcement of Alimony Orders in Other States or Out of the Country

If you move to another state, can your wife enforce the alimony award? Yes. All states have now enacted the *Uniform Reciprocal Enforcement of Support Act*. This act was designed to deal with the problem of enforcing alimony and child-support obligations in other states. The procedure is simple. The ex-wife initiates the action in the state of her residence (called the initiating state). The court in the initiating state makes a finding as to the amount due. The finding is forwarded to the appropriate public official in the state of your residence (called the responding state). This official will have you served with an order directing you to appear in court. The responding state court enters an order for the amount due, and the public official in the responding state collects for the wife.

In addition, she can hire a lawyer in the state where you are and sue for her alimony arrearages.

Your ex-wife can also pursue you out of the country. In most cases the foreign court will enforce the American judgment as a matter of judicial courtesy (called "comity"). If you have assets remaining in this country, she can garnish them. The best way to protect yourself is to make arrangements in the U.S. for a lawyer or a bank to continue the payments to your ex-wife.

Don't be emotional about alimony and give away the lion's share of your goods to avoid it. Courts are *not* going to make you pay more than you can afford. If your circumstances change you can seek relief. Alimony can even be a tax advantage. But thanks to our farsighted legislators—and the Women's Movement—alimony is slowly disappearing. Today's man can take his saddlebags with him when he changes horses.

# CHAPTER VII

# Custody: Motherhood Is
# Not Enough

## A. What Is Custody?

One of the great sadnesses of divorce is the separation of child from parent. When a marriage ends, the children are awarded to the mother or the father. That parent is said to have custody. The other parent is granted visitation rights. This situation is not the natural way to rear children, but it is the best way society and the law have devised.

The parent who has custody will be expected to make the bulk of decisions regarding the child's upbringing, schooling and discipline. Naturally, both parents should make major decisions affecting the child's future, but the day-to-day problems are handled by the parent with whom the child lives.

## B. Guidelines Courts Use in Awarding Custody

The rule that all courts universally enunciate is that custody must be awarded to promote the best interests of the child. This is a fine principle. The difficulty lies in applying it, as each custody case is as unique as the people involved. Nevertheless, there *are* certain guidelines that courts have adopted in deciding custody disputes.

The first and obvious factors the court considers in awarding custody are the age and sex of the child. Ordinarily, a child of tender years will be awarded to the mother. A child of mature years, particularly a boy, is frequently awarded to the father on the theory that the father would be best able to educate and prepare the male child for a trade or a vocation. Similarly, courts often consider the girl of more mature years should be with her mother.

If an issue is raised as to the morals of one of the parents, the court must consider this factor. The difficulty is that sometimes the court gives more weight to the alleged immoral conduct than to the ability of the parent to perform as a parent. The obvious example is the wife who has committed adultery. Some courts have been known to give custody to the father, even though the mother, in spite of her indiscretion, might be better qualified.

The single case of adultery should be distinguished from flagrant promiscuity. The woman who has one live-in boy friend after another is not acting in the best interests of her children and certainly should not have custody.

If the child is of sufficient age to have formed an intelligent judgment about his custody, his choice will be considered by the court. Obviously, a court is going to give greater weight to the strong wishes of a sixteen-year-old than to the vague expressions of a ten-year-old. A few states require that the court comply with the child's wishes if the child has reached a prescribed age, usually fourteen. However, in most states the court is not bound by a child's wishes, for the child is frequently still too immature to make such a judgment.

It is a common phenomenon for a child of, let's say, sixteen to be indulging in what psychologists call parental revolt. The child will become attached to one parent and express undying hatred for the other. The parent who is more permissive is frequently the one for whom the teen-ager expresses a preference. I recall one case where the sixteen-year-old daughter was quite determined that she wanted to live with her father. She was so adamant that the court finally awarded the father custody. What the daughter really wanted was complete freedom from parental supervision. She wanted to see boys on a less supervised basis, to have friends over at odd hours, and to be independent. The father wanted this kind of living for himself. With the daughter underfoot, he spent most of his free time away from the apartment. The result was that the sixteen-year-old had the desired freedom. She soon discovered it wasn't all that much fun. The happy ending occurred six months later when she decided she really wasn't ready to take on the world. She returned to the more supervised and secure atmosphere of her mother's home.

Race is rarely a factor in awarding custody. It is a delicate, if not distasteful, subject and suggests a certain kind of prejudice we have been trying to eliminate in this country. A few cases involving custody of the children of white and black parents have considered the racial differences in awarding custody. One case awarded custody to the black parent on the theory that the child would be less subject to racial prejudice than he would be by living with a white family. The solution to this problem is to exclude race as a relevant factor in custody disputes and place the child with the parent whose affection and care will best serve that child.

Religious beliefs can also be a factor in custody. Continuity of a child's religious training is desirable. Courts have sometimes inquired into the religious background of the parties on the assumption that a deeply felt religious belief is the attribute of a good man. Today such notions strike us as somewhat naïve, if not archaic. Certainly it does not follow that regular church attendance proves that one is a good parent. Similarly, it does not follow that a person without deep religious convictions is unfit to be an affectionate and successful parent.

Courts have not attempted to discriminate between religious beliefs and place a child with a parent whose religion is the better-known. If, however, the custodial parent's faith forbids recourse to medical care, the court will sometimes impose conditions in the custody order insuring that the child will receive medical care when he needs it.

If parents enter into an agreement, before their marriage, that the children shall be raised in a particular religious faith, such agreements are not grounds for awarding custody. Furthermore, enforcement of such an agreement would be unconstitutional as a violation of the prohibition against respecting the establishment of a religion. While bigotry may not be entirely dead, it can be said with some assurance that courts have considered religion as a factor in very few cases.

The increase of faddist religious cults might prove to be an exception to the general rule that courts do not consider religion an important factor in awarding custody. Some of the cults make extreme demands upon the time, eating habits and living arrangements of their adherents. If a certain sect requires its members to live in a commune under primitive conditions where sexual mores are lax, courts may well determine that such physical and moral atmospheres are not in the best interests of a child. I know of at least two cases where the mother gave up custody when she embraced one of these avant-garde religions rather than face a court battle over custody.

We sometimes congratulate ourselves in thinking that unpopular political or social views do not disqualify a person for having custody of his children. Indeed the question has rarely been discussed in our law reports. Nevertheless, there have been recent indications that the social views of a parent may be a factor. The acceptability or the unacceptability of certain social views is probably going to depend upon the court and the state or community in which the court is located.

A most recent and celebrated case was in Iowa. In that case, the mother was deceased and the father was living in Berkeley, California, with his second wife. He was a free-lance writer and photographer. The children had been living for some time with their maternal grandparents in Iowa. When the father applied to the Iowa court to regain custody, that court held that the grandparents were better suited to have custody of the children than the father. The court felt that the atmosphere of Iowa farm life was far more beneficial for the rearing of children than the father's somewhat Bohemian mode of living.

Obviously, if the court believes that the social views of one of the parents would be detrimental to the rearing of the child, this is going to be a serious factor in awarding custody. One can imagine a mother who is so liberated that she sleeps indiscriminately with men in an "alternate lifestyle" or commune. This arrangement may suit her social views, but the courts, fortunately, are not so liberated. They would be apt to place the child in a more stable setting.

In the case of an illegitimate child, custody, in most states, goes to the mother. The tendency in some states, such as California, is to give the father of an illegitimate child the right to custody upon the mother's death. Furthermore, recognition by the father of the child as his has the legal effect of legitimizing the child in many states.

## C. Problems of Single-Parent Custody

Although the court grants one parent legal custody, the other parent still has a strong say in the rearing of the child. When differences of opinion arise, it is to the best interests of both parents (and the child) to work out a livable solution. If none can be reached, the court may be asked to intervene.

Obviously, this is to be avoided whenever possible. Court contests are costly and often leave unspannable bridges between the parents.

The most common disputes in child rearing occur over the basic fundamentals of living. Because they are basic and grounded in tradition, they become personal battles in which the child's welfare is often forgotten. Consider these problem areas:

## 1. *Religion*

Most courts have held that the question of religious training may be determined by the parent with custody. In spelling out custody rights the parents should agree ahead of time to avoid later confrontations. If a court must intervene, this agreement may not be considered.

## 2. *Surnames*

A child in the custody of a mother who has remarried, will often take the stepfather's name. This is usually based on nothing more complicated than the child's desire to have the same name as his mother's and be like the other kids.

Most natural fathers resent this and will try to put a stop to it. When such cases have gone to court the decisions have varied from state to state. Some states have decided that the parent with custody has the right to determine the name by which the child shall be known. Other states have held that the father's name must be used, and the parent with custody must see to it. Such control can be more difficult when the child becomes older.

One case in which I was involved posed just such a problem. The children were teen-agers in their mother's custody. Their natural father was a flamboyant, internationally known figure whose life was dutifully chronicled in the press. The children, in an attempt to disassociate themselves from his antics, started calling themselves by their mother's maiden name.

In retaliation the father contended that this relieved him of the obligation to support them. When I took the mother's case to court, the court held that the name the children chose to call themselves did not relieve the father of his obligation of support. He sired them. The children had no choice. If his conduct alienated them, that is the personal and tragic penalty he must pay.

## D. When Custody Is in Dispute

Ideally, both parents will agree, before going to court, which parent should have custody. When they don't, we have those tragic facts of divorce called custody fights in which each parent demands custody and challenges the fitness of the other parent.

Custody fights bring out all the raw emotions, the neuroses, even the paranoia of the parties. When a father requests that the court award him custody, a wife considers this a personal slur upon her as a woman. It is at this point that the tigress, ever lurking in all women, charges forth fighting ferociously for what she feels to be her very life function. Her fear is that in awarding custody to the father she will be branded an unfit mother. *Most mothers fear this appelation above all others.*

Today, in most states, it is not necessary to show that the mother is unfit in order to award custody to the father. All that is necessary is to show that the best interests of the child are served by awarding custody to the father.

Sometimes a father will make custody an issue simply to upset the mother or for leverage in bargaining for a lesser alimony award or a better property settlement. In these cases the father does not really want custody. He probably wouldn't know what to do with the children if he got them. Nevertheless, the court is put to the task of examining the claims of the father. I always advise the father not to seek custody for such reasons. Only seek custody when you genuinely think the children would be better off living with you than with their mother.

In a custody dispute, as in other disputes in a divorce case, each side is expected to present the facts which he believes entitle him to custody. These facts should emphasize the factors already discussed. There is one great difference in a custody proceeding: the *social worker.* If it wills (and it usually does), the court can direct a social worker to investigate the backgrounds and habits of each parent, the future plans of each parent should he be awarded custody, and the opinions of neighbors, teachers and doctors.

The social worker's investigation has certain drawbacks. Their reports are based upon hearsay and rumor and sometimes less than objective investigation and judgment. Many social workers are over-worked and do not have time to make a thorough investigation. The training, skill, thoroughness and good sense of the social worker are crucial. Unless their reports are thorough and well done they can be dangerous. When the investigation is poorly conducted the job of the judge and the lawyers becomes increasingly difficult at the court hearing.

Another important fact to bear in mind is that even when the parents agree as to custody, it is not binding on the court. The court may set aside an agreement regarding custody and give it to the other parent. If the court feels that neither parent would serve the best interests of the child, it may bypass both parents and place the child in a foster home, or award the child to one or the other set of grandparents, or to another relative. The ultimate consideration is the best interests of the child.


## E. Disputes Between a Parent and a Nonparent

In the undivorced family the parents are entitled to custody of their children despite the fact that they may not be skillful, intelligent, or provident parents. The rationale for such a principle lies in the well-established belief that, for all their faults and mistakes, parents are generally better able to care for their children than strangers. In addition, there is a profound emotional bond between parent and child which the state and law must respect. These attitudes may be described as the doctrine of parental right.

When the divorce occurs, the court looks first, as

we have seen, to the suitability of the parents in resolving custody disputes. As a consequence, most courts have held that, as between a parent and a stranger, the parent has the right to the custody of the child unless the parent is clearly found to be unfit. A few states have been critical of this view and held that no one, even a parent, has the right to custody if the custody does not serve the best interests of the child.

In a custody dispute between a parent and a nonparent, the nonparent must present strong claims. In a case where the child has been in the custody of a relative or foster parent for a long time and the parent seeks to regain custody, the parent's claim will frequently be rejected on the ground that the child's welfare is best served by his remaining where he is. On the other hand, if the separation has lasted only a short time, the parent has a good chance of regaining custody.

In disputes between parent and nonparent the relationship the child has with the nonparent is a deciding factor. If the nonparent is a grandparent or a relative, his claim for custody would be stronger than that of a total stranger or an agency for child care.

There often exists a situation where a child is placed by a parent with a friend or relative on a temporary basis. Then, when the parent tries to reclaim the child, the person with custody objects. In such a situation the courts will look to the intention of the parties, the nature of the relationship of the child to the nonparent, and the degree of contact that the parent maintained with his child during the child's stay with the nonparent.

In a recent case in a dispute between the mother and foster parents, the California Supreme Court held that it was *not enough* that the court found the best interests of the child were served by his remaining with the foster parents. There must be a positive showing that an award of custody to the mother would have a detrimental effect upon the child. Note that the court did not say the mother must be found to be unfit, but merely that the award of custody to the mother would have a detrimental effect on the child. This distinction between *unfitness* and *detrimental effect* may prove to be as confusing to lawyers and courts as it is to the layman.

## F. Changing a Custody Order

A custody order may be changed or modified just as child support and alimony orders may be modified. If custody has been awarded to your wife and later you feel that it would be to the child's best interest for you to have custody, you can petition the court. But first make sure you are not simply on an ego trip. Don't hold up every little infraction that your ex-wife may have committed to justify your action. Consult a lawyer; he will be more objective than you.

If your lawyer advises you to seek custody, he will prepare the necessary papers. This is usually in the form of a motion to modify the divorce judgment which originally awarded custody to your wife. The next step, in most states, is the assignment of a social worker to investigate the respective claims of the

and incapable of disciplining and supervising this somewhat obstreperous brood. The court appointed a social worker, who made the customary recommendation that the mother have custody. The judge decided otherwise. The husband, unusually efficient, hired a housekeeper to run the home while he was at work. He organized the boys' time and convincingly showed that by awarding him custody *now,* a great many problems could be avoided later. To let the wife have the boys and wait until they ran her ragged, would work to no one's advantage. Ten years ago the wife in such a case would have automatically been granted custody.

State legislatures are enacting laws supporting this viewpoint. For example, in California the custody statute formerly provided that, all things being equal, a child of tender years should be awarded to the mother. That statute has been repealed, and the law now provides that the best interests and welfare of the child are *the* consideration in awarding custody regardless of the child's age.

The Women's Movement is another force that is dispelling the myth of motherhood. As more and more mothers march off to seek their future *outside* the home, children are being reared jointly, if not entirely, by fathers. I am beginning to handle divorce cases in which the fathers are "presented" with the children—like it or not.

In a recent divorce case I handled, the wife simply moved out and left the husband with custody of the five children. This trend is increasing. Many recently divorced men are finding their blessed bachelorhood exploded by the arrival of their teen-agers seeking bed and board.

The trend to do away with alimony has forced many ex-wives out into the job market. When a mother must work and struggle along on her wages plus child support, it's a great temptation to send the children packing off to Daddy. Why, Mother reasons, should *she* break her neck trying to make ends meet while her "ex" lives in bachelor splendor?

You might keep these factors in mind when you think you want custody. There is an old Indian proverb which goes: "Be prudent in your prayers, for your wishes may come true."

# CHAPTER VIII

# Child Support: If They Are Yours, Pay for Them

## A. What Child Support Is

Parents have a legal as well as a moral duty to support their children—legitimate or illegitimate. When the mother has custody of the children, the child-support payment is made by the father to the mother. However, if the father were to have custody and the mother were able to make a contribution toward child support, she should.

The child-support payment, together with the contribututution of the parent with custody, covers the normal needs of the child: food, clothing, shelter, education, medical and dental care.

The fact that the mother with custody is receiving child support from the father does not absolve her from making her contribution to child support if she is able to do so. In deciding the child support the father must pay, the court also considers the mother's resources. Remember also, the child support obligation is *not* dischargeable in bankruptcy.

## B. What Child Support Is Based Upon

Child support is usually part of the divorce judgment. It is based on the ability of the father to pay. Obviously, a father of wealth is going to be ordered to pay more than a salaried man of modest means. But both must pay—for the father's sake as well as the children's.

It is important to remember that the parent with custody cannot waive the child's right to support from the other parent. A husband and father cannot give the wife a larger proportion of the property and absolve himself from child support. The wife may waive alimony, but she cannot waive the child's right to support. Many husbands are confused by the distinction between alimony and child support. Remember that alimony is support for the wife. Child support is what it says it is—support for the child.

When a mother remarries, the earnings and resources of the stepfather are not a factor. He has no legal obligation to her children. The natural father cannot seek a reduction in his child-support payments based upon the stepfather's earnings. If the stepfather wishes to contribute to the children's support, he certainly may. (We can imagine what would happen to his domestic tranquility if he didn't!)

The second factor the court considers in awarding child support are the needs of the child. A baby does not require the food or clothing of a teen-ager. Courts know this and are mindful that the older a child becomes the more expensive he is to maintain.

Special needs of the child must also be considered. The handicapped child, the child needing psychological or educational help, has a right to additional support. In such cases both parents should make special efforts to meet these needs. In most communities federal, state, county and special-aid help are available to parents with these extraordinary expenses. If you are the father of a handicapped child, check into the governmental aid programs that are available.

The illegitimate child is eligible for the same support help from the father. The law varies from state to state, but the Anglo-American juridical system recognizes the responsibility of the father to support all his children—regardless of their legitimacy.

A third factor, and one I suspect that shall take on increasing importance as the goals of the Women's Liberation are realized, are the abilities and resources of the mother. As already stated, the mother has an obligation to contribute to her children's support. If she is earning a good income or is independently wealthy, the court is not going to strap the father with the entire burden, particularly if he has moderate means. The court will shift more of the obligation to her.

## C. Those Extras

### 1. *Fact and fiction*

Not all needs of the children are real needs. There is a type of mother who, at the expense of what's best for the child, will be forever requisitioning the father for additional funds. Learning to distinguish necessary from unnecessary medical expenses is one concern. Children do not need to go to the doctor every time they have the sniffles or an earache. Some children need orthodontic work; some don't. If your ex-wife says Billy has to have braces—and you don't think so—you have the right to take him to a dentist of your choice. Often getting braces represents "what everybody else is doing."

Then, there are psychiatric bills. I have heard more than one neurotic wife say, "Because of our divorce the children need psychiatric help." I am *not* prepared to dispute that this may indeed be true in some cases, but *not* in most. More often, it is one or the other or both of the parents who need the help. My experience, and those of my colleagues, has been that children are amazingly resilient and adaptable. Once the divorce and the fighting are over, children adjust very well.

I once had a client, a very successful businessman, who was married to an extremely neurotic woman. She had been going through analysis for a great many years. Her husband and I were skeptical as to the good it had accomplished. When the inevitable divorce became a reality she wanted an open-end medical provision for the children. He (nice guy) was inclined to go along. I advised against such a provision and pointed out that she would have the children undergoing psychiatric care for years, following her pattern. The husband agreed with this advice. My fears were well founded, as she tried time and again to obtain additional child support for this purpose. Had we not put a limit on her spending, my client would surely be less wealthy than he is today.

In an open-end medical and dental provision the husband simply agrees to pay for all medical and dental expenses without bothering to limit them as to dollar amounts. This is not a good practice in any relationship.

## 2. *Extraordinary medical expenses*

Extraordinary medical and dental bills that are genuine are another matter. Your ex-wife can bring you into court and force you to pay them if you have the money. As a safeguard I advise husbands to obtain medical and dental insurance to protect themselves and their children from the unforeseen. Group medical plans are available. Frequently you can obtain one through your employer or your union. By all means make arrangements to get health insurance somehow, somewhere.

## 3. *Life insurance for the benefit of the children*

If a father dies before his children reach adulthood (and this is now eighteen for most purposes), a child has a claim for support against his father's estate.

If the father remarries and has a second family of small children, his death can work a double hardship on the second family. Therefore, I recommend that a father obtain life insurance for the benefit of his minor children. Upon his death the insurance payment is a substitute for the children's claim for child support against his estate. The exact amount of life insurance will, of course, depend upon the size of his estate and his ability to pay the premiums. It is a factor that he should weigh carefully with both his attorney and his insurance broker. Insurance is also extra protection for the child, as it can be used for his education in the event of the father's early death.

### 4. *Higher education*

Before a child reaches his majority, the father is under obligation for the child's education. If a child is anxious to go to college, the father should make every effort to help. If he has the means, but does not do so, the mother could well prevail in court on a motion for modification to require the father to pay for higher education.

However, a college-age child is usually past his majority. The divorce court no longer has authority to order the father to pay for higher education. Knowing this, a mother will try to have funds for college written into the Separation Agreement (see Chapter X). If the father agrees, this promise can be enforced in court. But even an agreement to pay is limited by the father's means. He can only be forced to contribute what is reasonable.

### 5. *Where to draw the line*

Most fathers want their children to have everything. This is part of the American Dream. When a man does not have custody, he feels a need to make up to the children in some way. He wants to show the children that he still cares for them. Material things become offerings of affection.

As delightful as the children may find this, it is not the best thing for them. Attempting to give a child everything could be disastrous for you financially. More importantly, the result could spoil the child irreparably. Be on guard that your ex-wife doesn't entice you into buying luxuries you can't afford.

Private schools, summer camps, lessons of all kinds—music, dancing, tennis—come under the heading of "optional expenses." You should clearly state the limits; otherwise your ex-wife may spend and spend all "for the sake of the children." Furthermore, giving children too much can instill in them a false sense of values. They may come to expect luxuries for the rest of their lives.

One area of confusion concerns child-support payments when the children are visiting you. I always advise fathers not to reduce or eliminate the child support when the children visit—even for six weeks in the summer. A good portion of the ex-wife's expenses for the children are continuing—mortgage payments, taxes, home insurance—whether the children are living at home or are temporarily with you. Give her this break. Don't give her the chance to call you cheap when it comes to child support.

### D. Income Tax Aspects of Child Support

If you contribute over 50 per cent toward the

support of your children, you may claim them as dependents on your federal income tax return. If you have a separation agreement with your ex-wife, make sure the agreement states that you, and not she, will claim the children as dependents. I've seen parents get into trouble with the Internal Revenue Service where both claimed the children as dependents. One party or the other is going to lose out in a tangle with the IRS. Make sure it isn't you.

## E. When Child Support Terminates

Child support terminates when the child reaches his majority. In most states this is now eighteen. Additionally, child support usually terminates upon the marriage of the child. This is particularly true of the female child.

Child support also terminates when the child becomes self-supporting. This frequently occurs when he goes into the service or obtains a full-time job.

The obligation also terminates in the unhappy event of the child's death.

## F. How to Terminate Child Support

In most states child support automatically terminates by the happening of one of the conditions previously mentioned. In some states it is necessary to apply to the court to obtain an order terminating the obligation. Further, the child-support obligation may terminate upon the happening of one of the conditions above or pursuant to a written agreement with your ex-wife.

If one of the conditions for termination has occurred and your ex-wife hasn't signed a written agreement with respect to termination, have your lawyer get a court order. All you and he simply prove is that one of the conditions giving rise to termination of child support has occurred.

## G. How to Reduce Child Support

If you attempt to reduce child support, you must show a change of circumstances, similar to what you must show in reducing alimony. The change may constitute a reduction in your income or resources. The change may consist of increased income or increased resources of the mother. Conceivably, change of circumstances could constitute a change of circumstances of the children. It may be that their grandparents have set up a trust fund for them which supports them, or that they have come into an inheritance.

The procedures for reducing child support are similar to the procedures we discussed in reducing alimony. A motion is brought in court by your lawyer, and at that time you must prove the change of circumstances. A court hearing is then held and it is determined if there has been a sufficient change to justify a reduction of child support.

If you and your ex-wife have verbally agreed to a reduction in child support, get this agreement in writing and get it confirmed by a court order. Your lawyer will know how to handle this. Remember also, just as child support can be reduced upon showing of a proper change of circumstances, it can be increased upon such a showing. As the children get older and inflation continues, the increase is more likely to be granted than the reduction.

## H. How the Ex-Wife Can Enforce the Child-Support Order

If you don't pay your child support your ex-wife can cause you trouble. Frequently a court will be lenient on a man who fails to pay his alimony. But when a man fails to support his children, judges, with righteous indignation, will sock it to him.

Your ex-wife can ask the court to find you in contempt for failure to pay, and the consequences could be jail. She must prove:

1. that you knew about the support order (obviously you did);
2. that you have the ability to pay (do you?);
3. that you willfully failed to pay (did you?).

To avoid being found in contempt, always pay to the very best of your ability. Make sure that it is the best of your ability and not that you are giving priority to other things. The court won't send you to jail if you can show that you have made all reasonable efforts to pay. Remember, your child-support obligation comes before all others. Child support has priority over all other debts and is not dischargeable in bankruptcy.

In addition to the contempt process, your ex-wife can have her lawyer execute on your assets, including your bank account. She can also garnish your wages (a procedure which will not endear you to your employer or make for stable employee-employer relationships). She can have her lawyer get a court order directing your employer or other people who may owe you money to pay her directly.

If you move out of the state or out of the country, child-support orders are still enforceable. Your ex-wife can hire a lawyer in the new state who simply files the judgment in the state where you live. She can enforce that judgment in the new state the same as it would have been enforced in the original state. The process is a bit more cumbersome if you go to a foreign country. However, most foreign countries will enforce a child-support order of an American state.

In addition, all states have now adopted the *Uniform Reciprocal Enforcement of Support Act*. Under this act the wife begins the motion in the state of her residence (called the initiating state). The court in the initiating state makes a finding as to the amount due. This finding is then forwarded to the appropriate official in the state where the father lives (called the responding state). This official serves the father with an order directing the father to appear in court. An order is executed directing the father to pay. The public official collects for the wife. The procedure is relatively easy, efficient and effective.

Remember, your children are your children—no matter where they live. You brought them into the world; they had no choice in the matter. You should contribute to their support to the very best of your ability. This obligation should and does take first priority. If you remember this and perform faithfully, you won't get into any trouble. At the same time, don't be a patsy. You are not doing your ex-wife or children any favors by giving them a blank check. Children need to know limits; they need to learn to live within their means; they need to know the value of money; and they need to know the joys of earning their own money.

One final word. Some fathers, out of vindictiveness, give the child-support money to the child rather than the mother. This is wrong; the money is to be given to the mother. She is the one with the obligation to feed, clothe and shelter the child.

# CHAPTER IX

# Child Visitation: Christmas Eve in the Airport

## A. The Importance of Visitation

No father enjoys the thought that a court will determine when he can—and cannot—see his children. But when custody of his children is granted to his wife, this becomes the exact function of the Visitation Order. It frequently spells out in dates and hours, holidays and vacations, the blocks of time when his children will be his alone.

This means a father will have limited and infrequent access to his child. Because of this, it becomes imperative that his time with them be utilized and well spent. It is during these periods that his relationship with his children *must* be developed, if one is to develop at all.

Visitation periods are more often than not strained as well as artificial. The time is an unpleasant reminder to the father and the children that their relationship is different from that of the usual family. These thoughts can be painful—both to the child and the father.

Aside from the strained and artificial nature of visitation, the father's role is a hard one. He is not their constant supervisor and yet he must exercise supervision and discipline while they are with him. He must resist the temptation to be only a good-time pal to the children and must carefully walk the plank between playmate and professor. He must give his children every opportunity to discuss their problems and their plans for the future. He must have a ready ear so they will want to come to him for advice. This is not easy for a full-time father. It is a demanding task for the weekend father.

Because of the hardships of visitation, a father may feel that the children would be better off without him. This is a cop-out. Think of all the families who are separated by jobs in the armed forces. A part-time father has a great deal to offer, and failure to exercise his parental obligation is robbing the children—and himself.

## B. Reasonable Visitation Rights

A father can expect that the courts will be extremely fair in dealing with visitation rights. Most visitation orders simply state that the father shall have reasonable visitation rights. This type of order relies on the goodwill of both parents. It is based on the mother's sense of fair play and the father's sense of responsibility. In other words, the court is saying that the mother will not unreasonably withhold access to the children, and the father will not upset the routine of the mother's household.

The difficulty here is with the word *reasonable*. One of the parents may feel that the other would not be "reasonable" and insists that the court set forth in detail the visitation rights. When the visitation rights are delineated, they usually provide that the father may take the child for a certain part of the summer— two weeks, one month, six weeks—depending on the age of the child. The father will be granted certain holidays or parts of holidays, specified weekends, and overnights.

No matter how reasonable parents think themselves, holidays can be gruesome. Christmas in the airport is not fun for anyone. Yet, I've known courts to order that feuding parents divide Christmas, meaning that at noon on Christmas Day one parent must relinquish the children to the other. I have known cases where this meant the children spent all of Christmas Day sitting in an airplane traveling between parents. The legal rights of both parents were observed, but nobody remembered to think about the children.

## C. Visitation Do's and Don'ts

### 1. *Making plans*

Getting ready to pick up the children from their mother involves making plans. She will need to know when you are arriving, how you want the children dressed, when you will be returning. *Do* make these plans with her. *Don't* try to handle the plans with the children hoping they will remember to tell their mother.

## 2. *Weeknight visitation*

Often a father requests that the children have dinner with him one night during the week. *Do* take the children's age into consideration. If they are small, make it an early dinner. If they are teen-agers with homework to do, *don't* take them to the movies. It may be your right, but it's up to you to fit into their schedule.

## 3. *Weekend visitation*

In fairness to the children, let them know ahead of time which weekend they are to visit you. If you are taking them out of town skiing or sailing, give them time to get their gear together. *Do* be honest with your plans; don't spring a surprise visit on them at the last minute. *Don't* be unreasonable if they have made other plans. As children grow up, their lives become more involved. It is unfair to expect a boy to give up a Little League game or a girl a special party. Letting everyone know your plans ahead of time allows them to make theirs.

## 4. *Summer visitation*

Summer visitation will allow you more time to develop your relationship with your child. Of course it is always pleasant to take your child on your vacation wherever it may be—the mountains, the seashore, a foreign country. But remember that summer vacation should not be all fun and games.

*Do* let your child see you go off to work every morning and participate in the details of your everyday life. He will learn an appreciation of what you do and how you earn your living.

*Don't* treat your child as a guest. Ask him to perform certain chores around your house. If the child is old enough to have a summer job, helping him get one is part of your responsibility. Combine fun and a good time with normal living. If you help your child develop a sense of responsibility, you will have made him an invaluable gift.

## 5. *Attitude toward visitation*

When your child is with you, concentrate on him and his needs. *Do* try to make him feel that you are concerned about him. But too much fussing over a child will make him feel that divorce has made him different, that divorce has harmed him.

The biggest mistake fathers make is to criticize the child's mother to him. If your child brings up the subject of his mother, show polite interest. After all, she was your wife and is a vital part of your child's life. Above all, guard against criticizing the mother. You will be the one to suffer in the long run.

The second biggest mistake fathers make is to give the child the third degree about the mother's activities. *Do* ask about the child's activities but *don't* ask about his mother's. What she does now is not your concern. How she lives her life is strictly up to her. Furthermore, you are putting the children on

147

the spot again and making their visit unpleasant. Kids want to love *both* their parents. So help them to do it.

## 6. *Conduct during visitation*

If you are living with a woman, *do* suggest she make other plans while the children are with you. Their age should be your guideline. *Don't* flaunt your affair to hurt their mother or impress your older children. You are a father who must set proper examples. Remember, children will accept "far out" behavior in others that they will not tolerate in their parents.

If you are living with another man, *do* watch your actions. He can certainly be involved in your activities, but *don't* force knowledge upon children that they are unable or unprepared to accept. Allow your children to think of you as naturally as possible. Becoming a freak in their eyes is not striking a blow for freedom.

## 7. *Rules during visitation*

One of the great temptations of the part-time father is to thoroughly spoil his children. Divorced parents carry an enormous load of guilt. One way for you to ease the burden is to cater to the child's every whim. This, of course, is good for no one. *Do* make rules for your children. Setting guidelines shows how much you truly love them. *Don't* let them treat you like a patsy.

Don't be a "no show." Telling the children or their mother that you will pick them up at a certain time and failing to show up, or habitually arriving late, damages your relationship with your children. Further, it gives the mother a chance to say to them, "Your father is so unreliable. He really isn't interested in you. He only comes around to annoy me."

## 8. *Competition between parents*

You are not in a contest with your ex-wife to see who is the better parent. You are not out to prove to your children that you love them more than their mother does. You are not conducting a spend-a-thon to show your children who's the champion in their lives. You are an adult man who is trying to do the best for his children. *Do* remember your children's birthdays and special holidays. *Don't* turn visitation into Olympics of overindulgence.

## 9. *When children become con artists*

Despite all the advice, it is not uncommon for divorced parents to compete for the affection of their children by buying the little ones all kinds of luxuries. Children are quick to perceive the competition and to take advantage of it by playing one parent off against the other.

"You are so mean. You won't buy me the dress I need, but my father will," pouts the teen-age daughter to her mother.

"Gee, Mom says she can't afford to buy me the tennis racket I need," whines the high-school boy to his dad.

Don't be conned. Talk it over with the mother.

Present a united front to the kids. Spoiling them might help your ego but it harms the kids.

## D. What to Do When Your Ex-Wife Discourages Visitation

The mother who discourages visitation presents a classic problem. Frequently she is neurotic, which complicates the situation. I find it very strange that a woman can marry a man, live with him, have children by him and suddenly, when divorce occurs, consider him no longer fit to see his children.

The most extreme case I recall was a battle between divorced parents that lasted for twelve years. The woman was pathological about visitation. She went into a tantrum at the very idea. To avoid her mother's wrath the little girl pretended to hate her visitation with her father. She would cry and scream and force her father to drag her from her mother's house. Once with her father, she would enjoy herself enormously. After she was returned home she would invent stories of how unhappy she was with her father, how she missed her mother, and how she never wanted to visit him again.

In this particular case, the parents divorced over the wife's infidelity. Consumed with guilt when her lover failed to marry her, the wife transferred her anxieties to her ex-husband by making him an ogre in her fantasies. She envisioned him completely unsuited to visit their daughter. Not only was this a tragedy for the daughter but it was a wasted life for the mother.

For the next twelve years this woman devoted her

150

time and energy fighting the father's attempts to exercise his visitation right. A psychiatrist was called into the case. It was his feeling that a bond still existed between mother and father and that the fight over visitation was the way they kept it alive. Neither was able to remarry and have a new family. They seemed to prefer the macabre ritual of court battles. The greater tragedy, of course, is the child who is caught in this psychotic performance. Do you wonder what kind of a woman this little girl will become? Does she have a chance of becoming anything but the neurotic her mother has raised her to be?

Trying to work with a mother who discourages visitation is difficult. Don't try to work out the problem through money. You can't withhold the child-support payment. This is not fair to the child. You should not withhold alimony payments either, as this money also helps the child.

Your recourse is in the courts to set specific visitation times. If your ex-wife fails to abide by the court order, you can have her brought into court for contempt. This can be very expensive for her. Most women "learn" to co-operate.

The contempt procedure represents the hard line and it makes for resentment, bitterness and revenge. I always recommend that you apply the soft approach first. Don't lose your temper. When your wife puts hurdles in your way, be polite and show her you intend to co-operate. If you have more than one child, ask to take all of them. She will soon see the advantages of letting you take the children. She is then free to have a social and private life of her own.

There are other advantages to the wise mother who encourages visitation. You can subtly point them out. If she co-operates, when you ask to switch weekends, help her with those "extras" for the children. Send all the kids home in new sneakers or pay the entire orthodontic bill instead of your required half. Sometimes a sure-fire way to get the kids is to pay their transportation *both* ways.

## E. Who Controls Visitation Activities?

Some mothers think they can control what their ex-husbands do with the children during visitation periods. They can't. Obviously, you shouldn't do anything with the children that endangers their health. Nor should you expose them to an immoral situation. If you take the kids to your apartment, be sure you're sleeping alone when they come bouncing into your bed Sunday morning.

You certainly may, however, take your lady friend out to dinner with your kids. Your ex-wife cannot dictate your social life. You may take her on trips with the children as long as proper sleeping arrangements are observed. And proper sleeping gear. I represented a woman who lodged a stinging protest when her ex-husband's girl friend flounced about his apartment in a flimsy baby-doll "shortie." It wasn't the husband's male reflexes she worried about but her teen-age son's. He came home from Dad's in a high pitch of excitement that unnerved the entire household.

## F. Out-of-State Visitation

Visitation out of state presents a more complicated problem. Because of the travel expense, these visitations are longer. Even if the arrangements are complicated, always see your children whenever you can. For some cases it might be easier, and less expensive, if you traveled to where they are. Don't let distance rob you—or them—of the privilege of being a father.

## G. Renewing Visitation Rights After Lapse

Many fathers going through the bitterness of a divorce want to stay as far away from the ex-wife as possible. As a consequence, they don't see their children for any number of reasons. Some fathers feel ill-equipped to handle very small children. Some fathers feel such guilt they are unable to face older children.

If you have been sporadic in your visitation rights or even let them lapse, you still have a right to renew those visitation periods. Start by writing your ex-wife a letter telling her you want to take the children out for dinner. Remember, if you have let visitation lapse, you are a near stranger to your children. Start with a short visit like a lunch or a dinner. As you re-establish yourself with your children, these visitations can be extended for longer periods.

If your ex-wife is unco-operative you can, through your lawyer, apply to the court to have your visitation rights set forth in detail.

## H. Rights of Grandparents to Visitation

Many states have enacted laws permitting grandparents and other relatives visitation rights. This is a salutary innovation. Grandparents still love their grandchildren and should be allowed to see them, even though their relative might not be the one with custody.

Like all good things, the rights of grandparents can be carried too far. I know of one case where the grandparents were extremely officious. Although the mother was raising the children properly, they disagreed with everything the mother did. They insisted upon taking the children every other weekend for the two full days. They attempted to undermine the mother's authority by telling the children that their mother was not raising them properly. They encouraged the children to defy the mother. Unfortunately, the judge, a grandfather himself, didn't realize the destructive influence the grandparents represented and ordered that the weekend arrangements continue. The result was that the mother and her new husband, a minister, were forced to leave the country. They took the children to Canada and established a new life away from the meddlesome grandparents.

## I. Torturing One Another Through the Children

Frequently the visitation procedure is the only personal contact between an ex-wife and an ex-husband. When the bitterness has not died, hatred, the psychologists tell us, takes the place of love. In this situation, whether hatred or latent love, the parties tend to use the children to punish each other. Try not to get pulled into this emotional trap. You have enough problems without that.

Let me repeat: Never disparage the mother to the children. First, the courts are adamantly opposed to such conduct. Secondly, it reflects more unfavorably on you than on the mother. After all, she was good enough for you to marry and become the mother of your children.

Let me also repeat: By exercising your visitation rights to the children you are encouraging the little woman to have a social life away from the children. This increases her chances for remarriage, which will get you off the alimony hook.


## J. Hidden Expenses of Visitation

There are certain hidden expenses of visitation. If, for example, you decide to take the children skiing, it's up to you to supply the gear. You shouldn't expect the mother to bear the expense of skis and parkas from her child-support money unless she and the children live in an area where parkas are normal wardrobe. If you decide to send the kids to summer camp, the cost of the camp is up to you. Don't subtract it from her child support. It was your decision, so you pay for it. But swimsuits, levis, sweatshirts and sneakers are her expense.

One ruse to be on guard against is the mother who will send the children to the father dressed in ill-fitting old clothes. This is an attempt to force the father to buy them new clothing. Don't fall for this trick. Call her and tell her how unkempt the children looked, but don't discuss it with the children. It could be embarrassing to them and it is their mother's fault, not theirs. If the mother complains that she doesn't have sufficient child support, point out to her that dressing the children as scarecrows is *not* the way to state her grievance.

If you decide to buy extra clothing for the children when they are with you, call their mother and ask her what they need. Of course, if they are teen-age girls, they will be happy to tell you—and tell you—and tell you.

Child-support payments should continue even when the children are visiting you. Most of the expenses of child support continue, whether the children are living in the house or not. Their rooms are there, the mortgage, the taxes and insurance still have to be paid. So grin and bear it.

## K. How to Modify Visitation Orders

A visitation order can be modified the same as custody, alimony and child-support orders. The procedure to modify visitation rights is much the same. You show the court that the visitation rights you propose are for the best interests of the children.

If your ex-wife has been unreasonable by withholding visitation or making it extremely difficult, your lawyer can bring a motion in court to specify the visitation periods. Don't sit back and let her attitude keep you from seeing your children. The court will always support you in this kind of quarrel.

In visitation proceedings the acrimony is almost

as great as in custody proceedings, so use all the little hints I have recommended to avoid going to court.

One final hint: Most judges are men. They will be inclined to give the father reasonable and fair visitation rights.

# CHAPTER X

# Property Division: What's Hers Is Hers; What's Yours Used to Be Hers, Too

It is important to make a distinction between alimony and property division. Alimony, as we have discussed earlier, is the payment for the support of the wife. It is tax deductible on the husband's federal tax return and chargeable as income to the wife. It ceases when the wife dies or remarries; it can be modified—that is, it can be increased or decreased. It can be paid for a specified length of time or for an indefinite period.

Property division, on the other hand, is a permanent division of the property of the parties. It is not increased or decreased. It is not considered part of the income or expense of either party. This distinction would seem elementary, but don't blame yourself if it is confusing to you. Many judges also seem baffled by the distinction.

The property settlement is usually made at the

time of the divorce. It is important to remember that the bare legal title of the property acquired by the spouse does not necessarily affect the real rights each may have in the property. Just because the property may be in the husband's name alone does not mean that the wife has no rights to the property. The same is true if property is in the wife's name alone, or in their joint names.

## A. How Property Is Divided

The statutes in various states set forth how the property should be divided:

### 1. *Community-property states*

Community property is that property acquired by either one of the spouses during the marriage other than that property acquired by gift, devise, or descent (i.e., gift or inheritance). Therefore, property which a party had before marriage, property which is given to him, and property which he inherited is his separate property. Furthermore, the normal increase of separate property (interest, rents, dividends) is separate property. All other property acquired by either of the parties during the marriage is community property.

In some community-property states the community property is divided equally upon divorce. In other community-property states the court attempts to work out an equitable division of the property at the time of divorce.

## 2. Common-law-property states

States which have not adopted the community-property system are called common-law-property states. In these states the division of property is based on the old English common law. Naturally, these states have enacted statutes drastically modifying the old English law. Consult your lawyer. He is your best guide as to the property-division laws in your state.

The statutes in the various states providing for property division usually employ vague terms that the division should be "just" or "equitable." Obviously this is not a very clear or definitive standard. It is, therefore, left to the parties and their attorneys to negotiate the property settlement, guided only by the statutory admonition that the result be fair, just or equitable.

## B. Adding Up the Assets

The law divides property into two major categories: real property and personal property. Real property is land or things attached to land, such as houses or buildings. All other property is personal property. It can be money, stocks, bonds, or more intangible things such as a right to royalties or a right to receive property at a future time.

The first thing to do when considering your property is to make a list. It should include:

1. Real property. Your home, mountain cabin, desert lot, seaside cottage or commercial buildings.
2. Stocks and bonds. All other forms of

securities, including unlisted stocks and securities.

3. Cash, checking accounts, credit union accounts, savings accounts, certificates of deposit, notes, and mortgages.

4. Retirement and pension funds. A lot of people overlook the fact that their pension fund has a value even if it represents a future, deferred or contingent payment. These benefits should be considered in dividing the assets of the marriage.

5. Closely held businesses, small corporations, partnerships and sole proprietorships. These assets can cause a lot of trouble in evaluating and dividing, but they do have value and must be considered.

6. The professional practice: medicine, law, dentistry, veterinary medicine, accounting, or engineering. These all have value and must be considered as an asset of the marriage.

7. Objects of art, antiques, various collections such as coins, stamps, paintings and tools.

8. Automobiles, trailers and boats.

9. Stock options and interests in profit-sharing plans.

10. Life insurance, annuities and endowment policies.

11. Social Security benefits and Kehoe Plan rights should not be overlooked.

## C. Evaluating the Assets

All assets must be evaluated. Stocks and bonds sold on a regular stock exchange or over the counter should be listed at fair market value. Stock in a company that is closely held and not sold on any stock market is frequently difficult to appraise. It may be necessary to hire an accountant or an expert in that type of business to examine the books of the company in order to obtain an opinion as to the value of the stock.

Stock options may or may not have a value. I recall one case where the husband had stock options in the corporation for which he worked. At the time of the divorce his option to purchase the company's stock was for more than the stock could be purchased on the open market. Furthermore, his option to purchase was for a limited time. After his option expired, the stock increased in value. His ex-wife went into court asking that she be given half the stock that he could have purchased when the stock option existed. Needless to say, she was turned down.

Real problems arise when you start evaluating a small business, whether it's a small corporation, a sole proprietorship, a partnership, or a professional practice. Many types of business and professional practices will generate a lot of money but have few tangible assets. As a rule, such businesses and professional practices are not readily salable. In such cases accountants, appraisers, and various experts will be employed by your attorney to determine a fair value of such a business or practice.

It may be necessary to have a real estate appraiser estimate the value of your property. It may also be necessary to have an expert appraise your antiques, art, coin and stamp collections. Furnishings, too, if they are of special value.

For furniture that is not antique, I suggest you put a low evaluation on it. It may have been expensive when purchased, but it is very difficult to get a good price in the second-hand furniture market. Sentiment has little resale potential.

## D. Who Should Get What

Most women with minor children want to keep the home and the furniture. The home, the nest, gives mother and children a sense of security which becomes all the more important in healing the emotional wound of a divorce. If it is financially sound, I generally advise the husband to accede to this desire. More often than not, the mortgage payments are less than it would cost the wife to rent a house or apartment for herself and the children.

However, there are times when the house would be too expensive for the wife to maintain on her alimony, child support and earnings. The best solution then is for the parties to sell the house and arrange to buy a smaller, less expensive one for the mother and children to live in.

Sometimes the house represents the major asset of the marriage and there is no other property that could be awarded to the husband to offset an award of the home to the wife. In such cases there are three possible solutions:

First, the husband may wish the wife and children to have the home outright. In return for his generosity, it may be feasible for the wife to waive alimony or at least agree to less alimony.

Second, the home could be sold and the proceeds divided in such proportion as to effectuate a fair, just and equitable settlement. Hopefully, there would be enough in the wife's share to allow her to purchase another home for herself and the children. The wise man co-operates with the wife in her effort to acquire a home because, as already stated, mortgage payments are usually less than rent and a home gives a woman and children a sense of security. This can make her more reasonable at the negotiating table and in the future. Remember, if you have children, you are going to be dealing with this woman for a long time. It is best to help her maintain a sense of security.

Third, the wife can be allowed to live in the home until the minor children are grown or she remarries. Then the house can be sold and the proceeds divided.

In cases where there are no minor children, the award of the home is usually not such a crucial issue. Still, most women want a house. Giving the wife the house is a generous and wise move, if you can afford it.

If the husband operates a business or maintains a professional practice, that asset should be awarded to him. The same holds true for any business or professional practice of the wife. Any property that requires judgment and management should be awarded to the one most able to exercise the business judgment or management ability.

Cash, stocks, bonds and assets that are liquid can be apportioned between the parties to offset an award of a business to the other.

While retirement and pension funds are important, the rules governing the fund may prevent them from being awarded to any other than the person whose retirement fund or pension plan it is. If the husband is paying child support or alimony he may need these funds to continue to make these payments after his retirement.

If the husband owns and operates a business so that other assets will not offset awarding the business to him, the wife could be given stock in it or a note, secured by the assets of the business. The husband can then make installment payments on the note. It should be remembered that even if the husband is making installment payments on the property division, these payments are not alimony and the fact should be made clear in a separation agreement.

Insurance and endowment policies are important to consider. Frequently the husband will want to keep the children as beneficiaries so that the insurance proceeds upon his death fulfill his child-support obligations. Less frequently the husband might want to maintain his wife as the beneficiary in fulfillment of his alimony obligations. In return, she should waive inheritance or any other claims against his estate upon his death.

Those items that have a real value, such as art, stamp or coin collections, should be taken into account and used as an offset against property awarded to the other. Obviously the person who is the chief collector should be awarded the collection. Your family heirlooms should be yours, and hers, hers. Gifts from relatives should be awarded to the person whose relative made the gift—even this is not always easy. I remember one ridiculous case where the parties quarreled as to who should have the wedding gifts, since presumably they were given jointly to the happy couple. The solution reached was to write a letter to each doner requesting that he indicate to which spouse he intended to make the gift. What an embarrassing position to put your friends in!

Now we come to the most difficult part of the property settlement—the sentimental trifles. I am continually amazed at what turns otherwise intelligent, personable people into irrational, greedy animals. Two cases come immediately to mind. One involved a certain set of steak knives. Both parties absolutely refused to give in to the other's demand of ownership. Obviously the cost in attorney's time exceeded the value of the set of knives.

The other case involved a husband whose wife took the blender when she moved out. (It had been in the husband's home prior to his marriage.) I represented the husband and it took a fierce struggle on my part to convince him to forget the blender. He wanted to hold up the entire property settlement (which was substantial and complicated) over the ownership of the blender. At one point he threatened to break into the wife's apartment to snatch it. It may sound very funny to you to read about such antics, but I can assure you they happen. Just be sure they don't happen to you. Recognize the emotion for what it is and don't be turned into an ogre by an inexpensive possession, no matter *what* it represents.

## E. Dividing the Debts

If you have sufficient liquid assets, it is smart to

pay the debts from the available cash, stocks or bonds. That way, both of you are starting with a clean slate. Of course, if one of the assets that is awarded has an encumbrance, such as a house with a mortgage, the party who gets the house assumes the mortgage. Similarly the party who gets the automobile assumes the loan on it.

If there are not sufficient assets to cover the debts, it is usually the husband who will be required to assume them. He is usually the one with the major earning power. In this case he should get compensation for assuming these debts when the assets are divided.

## F. How to Get the Lion's Share and Still Appear Generous

Husbands frequently ask me this question in one form or another. No one wants to appear greedy but there is a natural desire to keep what you've made— or at best a goodly share. And it can be done. Here are a few guidelines.

Start out by giving her all the sentimental stuff: the picture albums, the wedding presents, the bottle collection. Don't assume the attitude that you are "throwing them in." You are giving them to her because you know how much they mean to her. You are being manly and generous because you want to lessen the tensions. (Nothing smooths the way like presents.)

If you have other assets that can offset it, give her the house and the furniture. As I have said, women like to keep the home and will frequently allow a high valuation on it if they are allowed to keep it.

Make sure that both house and furniture are fairly evaluated, but try to get them as high as reasonably possible. You can argue successfully that real estate is appreciating greatly.

If you own a business or professional practice, keep it. This is what is going to generate the income and property for your future. If the business is individual or closely held or a professional practice, you can sincerely value these according to accepted accounting practices at fairly low figures. Such businesses and practices have little value without your being there to do the work.

If you do have a small business, try not to retain the ex-wife as a partner. It is better to give her a note and buy out her interest in your business. There are many reasons for this. First, you don't want her meddling in your business. But if she has an interest in it she has a legal right to look at the books and examine your business documents. Second, her meddling may have an adverse effect on your customer relations. Usually customers like to deal with one person and don't like someone else (particularly an ex-wife) interfering. Third, if you have partners, they probably won't want to be in a forced partnership with your ex-wife. Finally, it is usually the best practice not to have a business relationship with an ex-wife. Suppose you needed a business loan and the bank required her signature and she refused to sign. See what I mean? Buy her out even if you have to lower your standard of living for a while.

Frequently those desert, mountain and seaside lots are liabilities rather than assets. You probably

JOHN CARPENTER'S
# THE FOG

JOHN CARPENTER'S "THE FOG" A DEBRA HILL PRODUCTION
Starring ADRIENNE BARBEAU, JAMIE LEE CURTIS, JOHN HOUSEMAN
and JANET LEIGH as Kathy Williams

**R**

paid more than they were worth in the beginning, so let her have them at your cost or fair market value, whichever is greater.

Your basic strategy is to give her the items that have high *present* value, and keep the items with future potential. Be willing to sacrifice now to reap your rewards later.

Let me give you an example of the application of this principle.

I once represented a husband; let's call him Alan. Alan had a good and growing business from which he derived a salary of $80,000 a year. He also had a beautiful home, with an equity worth about $200,000; furnishings and paintings worth $50,000; a place in Palm Springs, valued at another $100,000; and about $250,000 in cash and securities. Alan and I concluded that it was best to give his wife, Carolyn, everything but stock in his business, which was then valued at about $800,000. Total community assets: $1,400,000. So he gave Carolyn the home, the furnishings and paintings, the Palm Springs white elephant, the cash and securities *and* a note for $100,000 payable within five years. He got all the stock in his business. Total assets to Carolyn: $700,000. Total assets to Alan: $700,000 (the business, less the $100,000 note). In addition, Alan gave Carolyn $3,000-a-month alimony for three years. For three years he strapped himself, but he paid off his alimony. Within four years he paid off his note (early). Five years after the divorce he merged his company with a large national concern for fourteen million dollars' worth of that company's blue-chip stock. Alan's settlement with Carolyn, who had no minor children, was generous, but he knew what he was doing. He had been willing to sacrifice the short term for the long term. Carolyn didn't do too badly either. With all her assets and a large income she met a lot of people. She remarried a wealthy man about the same time her alimony expired.

If you are in a sufficiently high income-tax bracket, you can bargain to give her more alimony and retain more property.

Take a somewhat modified example of Alan's case. Suppose a man has a one-half interest in a business with a net worth of $400,000, which pays him a salary of $50,000 a year. His other assets consist of an equity in his home, furnishings and cars, all of which total about $60,000. He can offer to give his wife all the other assets and a generous alimony of $2,500 a month if she will relinquish her rights to his business. He can successfully point out that he needs the income and salary from the business to pay her alimony; that it is impractical to sell his interest or to give her a direct interest because his partner would object. As we have already discussed, Uncle Sam will be paying for a large part of the alimony. This will please her and she will be able to live well while the alimony continues. A woman spending money and going places meets more people than the wife who is financially strapped. Remember, when she remarries you are off the alimony hook.

If you can get a cut-off date to alimony, do so. A big alimony (with a cut-off date) sounds terrific to women. Five years is tomorrow, but they think it's forever. *This* is how you keep your plumbing-supply business (or whatever business you may have). Offset the alimony by taking more of your expenses from the business. As a single man, take a small apartment and cut back. You don't need mortgage payments to have a hell of a good time. Get the wife thinking of *right now*. You think of the future. This is where a good lawyer with experience guides you to a better future. Meanwhile you have kept a substantial part of your property intact.

Paying more alimony (and thus giving less property) is not always what husbands desire. Some men would rather give more property and pay less alimony or none. Having the wife waive alimony has the advantage of reducing your fears that she will be living off you forever. It also eliminates her opportunity to have alimony increased at some later date. A reduced alimony or no alimony also encourages some women to remarry sooner. This situation represents an advantage to her; she can remarry and not worry about losing alimony.

Talk over both possibilities with your lawyer. He is in the best position to advise you.

## G. The Separation Agreement

The separation agreement is sometimes called the Property Settlement Agreement. I have even seen it called the Termination of Marriage Agreement. These are not technical terms and they have no precise definition. *Separation Agreement* is probably a more accurate description, because such agreements usually cover more than property division. The separation agreement is an agreement of the parties entered into after or at the time of separation. It is made in contemplation of divorce.

The separation agreement usually includes the following:

1. Agreement of the parties as to child custody and visitation;
2. Agreement as to child support and fringe benefits for the children such as college education and provisions for extraordinary medical expenses;
3. Agreement as to alimony and property division;
4. Agreements regarding future interests, such as stock options, life insurance benefits, health insurance provisions, retirement and pension fund rights.

The separation agreement usually includes the following general clauses:

1. That it will be enforceable by contempt;
2. That the parties will divide income tax refunds;
3. That new property discovered after signing the separation agreement shall be divided;
4. That the parties agree to the signing of documents necessary for carrying out the purpose of the separation agreement;
5. That one or the other shall pay attorneys' fees;
6. That each waives the right to inherit from the other;
7. That alimony does not survive the husband's death;
8. That it is made in contemplation of one or the other party's obtaining the divorce.

Remember, alimony provisions may state that

there shall be periodic payments or lump-sum alimony paid in installments. Careful distinction should be made between alimony, which has favorable tax consequences for the husband, and property division, which does not.

## H. Can the Separation Agreement Be Modified by a Court?

In another chapter we have discussed how child custody, visitation, child-support and alimony orders can be modified. The question often arises: Can a separation agreement which includes these provisions be later modified by a court?

The courts have almost uniformly held that public policy requires that they may look into questions of custody, visitation, child support and alimony because there is a public interest in these matters. Therefore, custody can be modified and changed from one parent to another, depending upon the best interests of the child. Similarly, child-visitation rights can be modified. Child support may also be modified and suited to the ability of the parents to pay and the child's needs.

Although a weaker cause exists for asserting the public interest in alimony, courts have generally held that public interest requires that alimony be modifiable.

Property division is usually not modifiable. In most cases the actual, tangible division takes place shortly after the separation agreement is entered into. It is final and each receives the property awarded to him.

When a wife has given up substantial property

rights in return for a higher alimony award, it would be unfair to let the husband, a year or two later, reduce the alimony. Similarly, the wife should not be allowed to increase alimony when the husband has surrendered to her more than her fair share of the property.

Many courts have found such separation agreements to be what they call integrated agreements. The alimony provisions could not be modified because they were an integrated part of the property settlement agreement. The question of what provisions of the separation agreement are modifiable and what are not modifiable is one that depends upon the laws of the various states and the particular way the property settlement agreement is drafted. This is a subject you should carefully discuss with your lawyer.

## I. Enforcing Separation Agreements

The separation agreement is a contract and can be sued upon as a contract. If the separation agreement becomes a part of the judgment for divorce, it can also be enforced as a judgment in a manner similar to the one we discussed in enforcing child support and alimony provisions. (See Chapter VIII on Child Support.)

## J. A Model Separation Agreement

Since the separation agreement is such a vital and sometimes confusing part of divorce, it may help to show you a sample. This is not an actual agreement and should not be strictly followed. It is offered mainly as a checklist of ideas.

The background for this agreement is the failure of the marriage of Betty and Henry Riley. The Rileys met and married in Rochester, New York, where they had both lived and worked for five years. Betty was only nineteen at the time of her marriage, but she became an excellent bookkeeper. Henry was twenty-five and an engineer. By the time Henry was transferred by his company to San Jose, California, they had managed to save $20,000. A year after the Rileys arrived in California, they bought a home for $40,000 and made a down payment of $10,000. Betty gave up her job as a bookkeeper. Shortly thereafter, their first child was born. Two years later their second child was born.

About this time, Henry's company wanted to transfer him again, this time to work as a consultant on a project in South America. Betty and Henry did not want to uproot the family or leave California. In addition, Henry always had a hankering to be in business for himself. He found a small electronics company that made parts for use in computers and other electronic equipment that were manufactured in the San Jose area. Henry purchased the company for $50,000, paying $25,000 down and giving the owner a note for $25,000, secured by the assets of the business. He had $15,000 in savings, and managed to get a second loan on his home for $15,000. The remaining $5,000 he used as operating capital in his new business. Henry worked night and day doing the engineering, production and management of the company. Betty acted as bookkeeper and did most of the paper work. It was hard going, but they prospered. After ten years they had paid off both the former owner of the business and the second mortgage on their home—all with interest. By then Henry was bringing home a salary of $50,000 a year and Betty had ceased to work at the plant. They bought a new and more expensive home for $75,000, paid $40,000 down and assumed a mortgage of $35,000.

For the past three years things have not gone well in the Riley home, however. Henry is still absorbed in his business, which demands long hours and all his energy to keep up with the changing technology in his industry. On the business trips Henry has to take, he works hard; he also sometimes plays hard. Betty, used to working and now having nothing to do, has started to drink too much. Betty's drinking has turned off Henry and he has found another woman. Betty and Henry tried marriage counseling, but it didn't work. They then agreed to a divorce.

In California the only grounds are incurable insanity and irreconcilable differences. Obviously the latter is going to be the ground relied upon. All of their property was earned during their marriage and is therefore community property. California law requires that the community property be divided equally unless the parties agree otherwise. Betty and Henry agreed to divide the community property equally.

The community assets consist of the following:

1. Stock in Riley Electronics. They own 100 per cent of the company. The company's net worth is $110,000.

2. Equity in the family home, now worth about $50,000.

3. Furnishings in the home worth about $3,000.
4. A 1972 Ford Station Wagon worth $1,200. (Henry's car is owned by Riley Electronics.)
5. Savings account in the amount of $20,000.
6. Checking account in the approximate amount of $800.
7. Life insurance polices with a cash value of $5,000.

They agreed that Betty should have the house, car, the furnishings, the savings and checking accounts—which total $75,000. In addition, she is to receive a note for $20,000 payable in five years (secured by stock of Riley Electronics), representing the difference needed to give her one half of the community property. Henry is to receive all of the stock of Riley Electronics and his life insurance policy (worth $5,000), which is to remain for the benefit of the children.

In addition, Henry was generous with child support, education and fringe benefits. He further agreed to pay Betty $1,500 a month alimony for three yeras. This seemed like a lot of money to give to Betty (and it is), but Henry knows that Uncle Sam will be paying over one half of it. Remember also, it's a 22-year marriage and Betty helped in the business. Furthermore, Betty will be living comfortably for three years. This should give her time to find a new husband.

Here is what the attorneys prepared:

### SEPARATION AND PROPERTY SETTLEMENT AGREEMENT

THIS AGREEMENT by and between Elizabeth Riley (hereinafter called "Wife") and Henry Riley (hereinafter called "Husband") is entered into on the date hereinafter subscribed and is predicated upon the following facts:

A. The parties hereto are husband and wife, having been married on June 23, 1953, in Rochester, New York.

B. There are two (2) minor children, the issue of this marriage:

Henry Riley, Jr., born March 19, 1959
JoAnn Riley, born February 19, 1961.

C. The parties desire to settle for all times their property rights and any and all claims each has or may hereinafter have against the other by way of property, support, or otherwise.

D. The property of the parties consists of the following:

1. Equity in family residence commonly described as 257 Hope Road, Los Gatos, California, having an approximate value of $50,000.

2. Furniture and furnishings located in said residence having an approximate value of $3,000.

3. Savings account #007 in Gatos National Bank, Los Gatos, California, in the approximate amount of $20,000.

4. Checking account #003 in New Hope Bank, Los Gatos, California, in the approximate amount of $800.

5. 1972 Ford Station Wagon automobile having a value of $1,200.

6. One Hundred per cent of the stock (1,000 shares) in the Riley Electronics Company, a California corporation, Sunnyvale, Califor-

nia, having an agreed net worth value of
$110,000.

7. Life insurance policy #247296 with Long life
Insurance Company in the face amount of
$75,000 on husband's life, having a cash
surrender value of $5,000; Sacred Life Insur-
ance Company policy #133320 in the face
amount of $20,000 having no cash surrender
value.

WHEREFORE, it is hereby mutually provided and
agreed as follows:

## I.  DIVISION OF PROPERTY

### A. Wife's Portion

Husband agrees to and does hereby convey,
transfer, assign, set over and quit claim to wife as her
separate property, all his right, title, and interest in
and to the following described property:

1. Equity in family residence commonly described as 257 Hope Road, Los Gatos, California.

2. Furniture and furnishings located in said
family residence.

3. 1972 Ford Station Wagon.

4. The monies in savings account in Gatos
National Bank, account #007, Los Gatos,
California.

5. Monies in checking account #003 in New Hope
Bank, Los Gatos, California.

6. Note in the amount of $20,000 bearing interest

at 7 per cent per annum, principal and interest payable in monthly installments of $396.10 or more, commencing January 15, 1976. A copy of the form of said note is attached to this agreement, marked Exhibit "A," and by this reference made a part hereto. It is understood and agreed that said note represents the value of wife's interest in the family corporate business commonly known as the Riley Electronics Company, after awarding to her the property described in paragraph I, A, items 1, 2, 3, 4 and 5 hereof. Said note shall be secured by 200 shares of the Riley Electronics Company. A copy of the form of said security assignment is attached to this agreement, marked Exhibit "B," and by this reference made a part hereof.

## B. Husband's Portion

Wife agrees to, and does hereby convey, transfer, assign, set over, and quit claim to husband as his separate property all her right, title, and interest in and to the following described property:

1. All of the shares outstanding (1,000) of the Riley Electronics Company, a California corporation, Sunnyvale, California.
2. Life insurance policy #247296 with Long Life Insurance Company in the face amount of $75,000 on husband's life, and life insurance policy #133320 with the Sacred Life Insurance Company in the face amount of $20,000 subject to the restrictions as hereinafter provided.

# II.  CUSTODY AND SUPPORT OF MINOR CHILDREN

A. The parties realize and understand that any agreement they make as to the custody of their minor children is subject to the approval of a court of competent jurisdiction, but subject to such approval, the parties agree it is for the best interests and welfare of the said minor children that custody be in the wife, subject to reasonable visitation rights in the husband.

B. Husband agrees to pay to wife as and for child support the sum of $200 per month for the support of Henry Riley, Jr., and the further sum of $200 per month for the support of JoAnn Riley. Said child-support payments shall commence on January 15, 1976, and shall be payable one half on the fifteenth (15th) and one half on the thirtieth (30th) day of each and every month thereafter until said child or children dies, becomes eighteen (18) years of age, becomes self-supporting, or until further order of the court.

C. Husband agrees to pay and maintain both said children as beneficiaries of his medical and hospital insurance plan or as beneficiaries of a similar plan until each of said children shall have attained his or her eighteenth (18) birthday or shall otherwise be deemed emancipated.

D. Husband agrees to maintain both said children as the beneficiaries of the aforedescribed life insurance with the Long Life Insurance Company during the period of the minority of the youngest of said children and for the period that either of said children shall be attending college, if they so attend.

E. College Education. In the event that said minor children are academically qualified, husband shall bear the direct expenses of college and post-college education of said minor children for so long as said children are seriously and profitably pursuing said studies, and further:

1. Husband shall have the right to be consulted with respect to, and to approve, the college or post-college institution selected by any of the minor children. Husband's approval shall not be unreasonably withheld.

2. Husband shall have the right to be consulted with respect to, and to approve, the expenses of each such child while so attending college or post-college instituion. Husband's approval shall not be unreasonably withheld.

3. Husband shall be furnished with the statements and bills for such education and may make payment directly to the college or to the post-college institution or to the child involved.

4. The foregoing obligations on the part of husband are expressly made dependent upon his demonstrated financial ability to bear such expense without substantially reducing or impairing his lifestyle and his ability to discharge and handle such other obligations for which he may then be obligated.

F. It is agreed between the parties that they will always conduct themselves in such a manner as to be conducive to the welfare and best interests of the minor children. The parties shall confer with each other on all important matters pertaining to the children's health, welfare, education, and upbringing with the view to arriving at a harmonious policy to promote the children's best interests.

G. Wife shall promptly notify the husband in case of a minor child's serious illness while in her physical custody. "Serious illness" shall mean any illness which may confine the child to bed for more than seven (7) days.

H. The parties agree that husband may declare the children as dependents on his federal and state income-tax return and that wife shall not declare the children as dependents on her federal and state income-tax return unless authorized by husband to do so.

## III. SUPPORT OF WIFE

A. Husband agrees to pay to wife as and for alimony the sum of $1,500 per month commencing January 15, 1976, and continuing one half on the fifteenth (15th) and one half on the thirtieth (30th) day of each and every month thereafter until December 30, 1978, at which time alimony shall cease and terminate.

B. Alimony shall also cease and terminate upon the death or remarriage of wife.

C. Husband agrees to maintain wife as beneficiary of the aforedescribed life insurance policy with the Sacred Life Insurance Company for so long as he shall be obligated to pay alimony to wife or to pay on the aforedescribed $20,000 note.

# IV. DEBTS

A. Husband agrees to pay the following debts:

1. Shop-Rite Department Store in the amount of $213.69.
2. Crisis Power Company in the amount of $46.53.
3. Dr. Amos Felt in the amount of $87.70.

B. Each party receives any property divided hereunder subject to any existing encumbrances thereon and agrees to hold the other party harmless of and from any liability, encumbrances or expenses imposed, suffered or asserted against the other party by reason of or arising from any encumbrances on such property transferred hereunder.

C. Neither party shall incur any indebtedness chargeable against the other or his or her estate from and after the execution of this agreement, nor contract any debt or obligation in the name of the other; and each party agrees to indemnify and hold the other harmless from and against any such indebtedness or obligation incurred or created by such indemnifying party.

D. Each of the parties hereby warrants to the other that he or she has not incurred any liability or obligation on which the other, or any of the properties transferred hereunder to the other party, is or may be liable, and each of the parties hereto agrees to indemnify and hold harmless the other party from and against any such liability or obligation heretofore incurred, and from all costs and expenses.

# V.   ATTORNEY'S FEES

Husband shall pay wife's counsel's fees and court costs in an amount not to exceed $7,500.

# VI.   GENERAL PROVISIONS

1. *Separate Character of Property Acquired.* The property of each party, whether or not acquired hereunder or pursuant hereto, shall be the sole and separate property of each party, and any and all property of any character and description hereafter acquired by either party shall be the separate property of the party acquiring the same, and the other party shall not have any right, title, or interest therein or with respect thereto.

2. *Complete Agreement.* It is expressly agreed between the parties hereto that this instrument is a full, complete and final memorandum of the agreement of the parties hereto, covering all matters in connection with the division of the property of the parties and all rights and claims of each and both of the parties therein or thereto, and of each and every claim of every character whatsoever one against the other, and that no agreement exists between the parties other than as herein specifically set forth; and it is hereby covenated and agreed by each of the parties with the other that he or she shall not assert or claim against the other any right or claim in or to any property of the other, except under the terms of this agreement and except as provided by the terms and provisions of this agreement.

3. *Agreement to Execute.* Each of the parties hereto agrees to execute and deliver to the other, or to any person to whom it may be necessary, or who may require the same, all deeds, bills of sale, assignments, consents, authorizations, waivers, and other instruments which may be necessary or required to carry out and give full effect to the terms and provisions of this agreement.

4. *Waiver of Right to Inherit.* Each of the parties waives any and all rights to inherit an estate of the other at his or her death, or to take property from the other by devise or bequest unless under a Will executed subsequent to the effective date hereof and except herein provided.

5. *Enforceable by Contempt.* It is further expressly agreed that if husband shall fail to fulfill his obligations under this agreement, wife shall have the right to bring contempt proceedings against the husband.

6. *Complete Disclosure.* Each party warrants to the other that there has been a full and complete disclosure of all the property held by each and that neither has made, without the knowledge and consent of the other, any gift or transfer of property within the period of the statute of limitations. If it shall hereafter be determined by a court of competent jurisdiction that either is now possessed of any property not set forth above, or that the one has made without the consent of the other any gift or transfer of property, other than as set forth above,

each party hereby covenants and agrees to pay to the other on demand an amount equal to one half of the fair market value of such property so transferred or conveyed.

7. *Equal Division*. It is the intent and purpose of this agreement to effect, as of the date of execution of this agreement, an equal division between the parties of all items of property owned by them. The parties acknowledge and agree that the division accomplished by the foregoing paragraphs of this agreement is such an equal division.

8. *Income Taxes*.

A. Husband agrees to indemnify and hold wife harmless from any and all liabilities which she may incur, or which may be imposed upon her or assessed against her or against any property she now or hereafter acquires by reason of the filing of any and all income-tax returns, federal and state, which she has heretofore signed and filed during the marriage of the parties, up to and including the return to be filed for the period ending December 31, 1975. Husband agrees to pay any assessment for deficiencies, penalties, interest, or the like, arising out of said returns.

B. Husband and wife agree to file joint income-tax returns, federal and state, for the calendar year 1975. Husband agrees to pay any and all income taxes upon all income of husband and wife for said calendar year.

C. Husband agrees to indemnify and hold wife harmless against any and all taxes, if any, arising out of, under, or by reason of the terms of this Property Settlement Agreement, except insofar as the provisions for alimony contained in this agreement.

D. If any deficiencies are assessed against husband and wife with respect to federal and/or state income taxes where the husband is under an obligation hereunder to indemnify and hold the wife harmless therefrom, and if the husband desires to defend against such deficiency assessment, he may do so at his expense.

9. *Indivisible Contract.* In the determination of the provisions of this agreement, the parties have given full and careful consideration to all present and future circumstances and events, including their respective ages, state of health and earning capacities, the ages and state of health of their children, the needs and requirements of their children and matters pertaining to their best interest and welfare, and their assets, properties, benefits and obligations, including those being transferred or assumed hereunder. The parties intend by this agreement that each covenant and promise to be performed by each of the parties shall be consideration for each covenant and promise to be performed by the other.

10. *Each Represented by Counsel.* The parties hereto acknowledge and agree that each has been represented in the negotiation and preparation of this agreement by counsel of his or her own choosing; that their respective counsel have been afforded a full and fair opportunity to examine and investigate the earnings, income, assets and matters

involved herein; that he or she has read this agreement and has had it fully explained to him or her by such counsel and is fully aware of the contents and legal effect hereof; and that this agreement is made and entered into freely and voluntarily by both parties, free from any duress, menace, fraud or undue influence of any kind, character or nature upon the part of the other.

11. *Interpretation.* This agreement is entered into in the State of California and shall be construed and interpreted under and in accordance with the laws of said State. Should any of the terms or provisions of this agreement or any clause or part thereof be held to be invalid, illegal or void, the terms, provisions, clauses or parts thereof held to be invalid, illegal or void shall be deleted from this agreement and the balance of the agreement shall subsist and be of full force and effect.

12. *Court Approval.* In the event that either party should hereafter at any time apply for and obtain a Judgment of Dissolution, it is the intention of the parties that this agreement be approved by the court and adopted as the full and complete determination of the property rights of each.

DATED: January 6, 1976

/S/ HENRY RILEY        /S/ ELIZABETH RILEY

HENRY RILEY, HUSBAND    ELIZABETH RILEY, WIFE

# CHAPTER XI

# The Role of the Lawyer:
# Yours, Hers, Ours

## A. Consulting Your Own Lawyer Can Sometimes Save You Money

Frequently a husband and wife feel they will save money if both go to the same lawyer. Their idea is that the lawyer will simply "draw up the papers" and they will sign them. This is all well and good when the parties are in total agreement as to all the items mentioned in this book—child custody, visitation, child support, alimony, and property division.

What this couple doesn't realize is that a lawyer must represent only *one* party. Although he may be the only lawyer involved and is drawing up the pleadings and separation agreement at the direction of both of you, he is actually acting for the party who is actively seeking the divorce. This is usually the wife. In this case you have the right to consult your own lawyer. Even if you have used the same lawyer to prepare the separation agreement, it is a sound precaution to go to another lawyer and have him look over the agreement.

If your affairs are complicated, if your debts are sizable, if your income is high, if your property is substantial, if your business is your own, if the marriage is of long standing, if you anticipate problems with child visitation, or if you anticipate problems in the future, it is wise to go to your own lawyer. Actually, any one of the above factors is justification—and an indication—that you should not proceed on your own. After all, protecting clients is a lawyer's primary function, and a divorce action is no exception.

To give you an example of the problems of using the same lawyer, consider the case of Beth and Edgar. Both went to the same lawyer, who drew up the papers and obtained their divorce for them. After three months Beth refused to let Edgar to take the children on his regular, agreed weekend. When Edgar went to the lawyer for help, the lawyer explained that while he got the divorce for them both, he technically represented Beth, as she was the party asking for the divorce. So what happened? Edgar had to hire another lawyer and take Beth to court. By the time this problem was settled, he had paid far more in attorney's fees than he would have had he had his own lawyer from the beginning.

## B. How to Select a Lawyer

Not all lawyers know (or want to know) much about divorce. The reasons are simple. Divorce is as hard on the nerves of the lawyer as it is on the parties. A divorce practice has many absorbing legal problems and many fascinating human aspects, but it frequently requires the added capacity of a psychiatrist without the added monetary award. Clients going through a divorce often treat their lawyer as they would their best friend. They make endless calls to his office over inconsequential matters, they heap their personal problems on his office staff, and they call his home late at night when they're lonely and distraught. A good divorce lawyer works very hard for his fees.

You are well-advised to choose a lawyer who is familiar with the practice—and problems—of divorce. The first criterion in selecting a lawyer is his reputation in the field. Certain lawyers have built their reputation to the point where their name is automatically mentioned with the word divorce. Others have a less public but nonetheless impressive reputation that is known to the legal community.

One way to select a lawyer is to ask a lawyer in another field whom he would recommend.

Another way is to consult a friend who was recently divorced. Who was his lawyer? Was he pleased with the result? One word of caution about this approach: No one is ever completely pleased with the results of his divorce. There can never be a clear-cut winner. Divorce is a negotiation, not a contest. And in a negotiation you give and you take. This is an occupational hazard a divorce lawyer must endure. Remember this, and listen to the criticism objectively.

A third way to select a divorce lawyer is through

the local bar reference service. Frequently lawyers will have indicated with their local bar association that they specialize in divorce cases. You can find the local bar association listed in the yellow pages of your telephone book.

## C. Lawyers' Fees

There are standards by which a lawyer sets his fees. As a minimum these fees are based upon the time spent on the case. Another criterion for an uncomplicated case is the customary fee charged by members of the local bar association. A difficult case—a case requiring unusual experience and skill—will attract a larger fee.

Favorable results are going to justify a larger fee. That doesn't mean simply the settling of the case. There are times when a lawyer saves his client a great deal of money in a divorce action, and as in any case involving large sums, the lawyer will rightfully expect a large fee. It is a rare case where the fees are exorbitant. If you feel your lawyer's fees are out of line, there is usually a client grievance committee of the local bar association that will investigate the matter.

Remember, most of your lawyer's work is done out of your presence. You really can't judge the time and effort he has spent on your case by the hours you have spent with him. In this respect the work of a lawyer is opposite to the work of a doctor. In most cases the doctor's work is done in the presence of his patient. In the case of the lawyer, most of his work is *not* done in his client's presence.

By all means discuss fees with your lawyer. He is anxious that you have a clear understanding of his work and the fee arrangement.

## D. What to Tell Your Lawyer

It's an old truism that you should tell your lawyer everything. Abide by it. This includes all the facts of your marriage, all the vital statistics of you and your family, all your income, all your wife's income, all your property, all her property, and all the family's property. Tell him about any special problems that you think might come up. The worst thing you can do is to withhold information from your lawyer. Tell him about your misdeeds, no matter how embarrassing it may be to you. Tell your lawyer what your wife might know about your misdeeds. He should never be surprised in court or when he goes to the negotiating table. (See Chapter I for further details as to what to tell your lawyer.)

## E. How to Help Your Lawyer

If you expect your lawyer to be the investigator, appraiser, accountant and psychiatrist, your fee is going to be higher. You will help him if you obtain as much information as possible without making him become the investigator. Provide your lawyer with all the details about the property, its location, the value you place upon it, how the property was acquired, what you paid for it. This includes everything from real estate to your savings accounts, your pension plans, and all the kinds of property mentioned in Chapter X. If you are living in a state where the marital misconduct of one of the parties is considered, provide him with the facts and not the fiction about her marital misconduct. Give the names and addresses and telephone numbers of witnesses so that your lawyer can talk to them and check out their stories. If you can provide him with the times, places and incidents of her misconduct, do so.

## F. How to Treat Your Lawyer

A man in the emotional throes of a divorce frequently tries to place his lawyer in a role no mere mortal can possibly fill. The client expects not just legal advice and representation, but a perceptive psychiatrist, a wise and sympathetic friend, a confidant for his anxieties and frustrations, sometimes a parent, and a tireless and invincible champion. Furthermore, when the client discovers that his lawyer is only mortal, he frequently becomes distressed and critical. No wonder the divorce lawyer, faced with such demands, often longs for the tranquility and security of a corporate or tax practice.

I don't mean to sound cynical about the role of the divorce lawyer. An intimate relationship does develop between you and your lawyer. You are telling him your innermost personal problems and you are asking him to handle the most precious things in your life—your children and their future, your home and your acquisitions. A mutual respect must develop. You must respect him not only for his skills as a lawyer, but as a person with good judgment who can help guide you in the personal and economic aspects of your divorce.

As you do and must respect your lawyer, don't tell him how to run the case. You are the client, he is the lawyer. He knows when to act and when not to act. He is fully aware of what to do when the time comes to act. Don't bug him every day on the telephone about your divorce. If you have something new to add, call him, but keep to the point. If you possibly can, it is best to put your thoughts into a letter. That way he has a permanent record with which to refresh his memory. Also, putting your ideas on paper forces you to discipline your own thinking about the problem.

Remember, your lawyer is a professional, but he is also a human being. He can become emotionally frustrated if you continually harass him. The gravest error is to compare your divorce with someone else's and then attempt to second-guess your lawyer. So many times I've heard clients say: "Why can't you get this for me?" No two divorces are alike any more than any two divorced persons are alike. If you compare your divorce with a friend's, it's only going to make one of you unhappy. You may become unhappy for reasons that might not be valid at all. You must trust your lawyer absolutely. If you don't, you have the wrong lawyer—and he the wrong client.

## G. How to Treat Her Lawyer

Your wife's lawyer is a professional. It is his duty

to represent her fairly. It is rare that a lawyer becomes so emotionally involved in the wife's cause that he loses all objectivity and becomes personally vindictive toward the husband.

Always be courteous when meeting with her lawyer. You will find that by being courteous he will have formed a good opinion of you. A lawyer respects a man who is courteous to his adversaries. If your wife's lawyer respects you, even though he's duty bound to represent her, you cannot help but have an unconscious ally working on your behalf.

Another thing to remember. Work through *your* lawyer; don't call *her* lawyer and pop off. It will not make him like you, and you will simply be giving him information he can use against you.

Don't blame her lawyer for your wife's misconduct, her bitchiness, her viciousness. If she is all those terrible things you claim she is, remember, *you* married her. Her lawyer didn't.


## H. How to Change Lawyers

You have a right to change lawyers, but don't do it often. I've known people to have as many as a dozen lawyers, with the result that none of them could do a good job. Changing lawyers is expensive. If you want to change, be sure the change is for the best. When you decide to change, have the new lawyer make the arrangements. He will see to it that all the papers, records, and exhibits are transferred in an orderly manner. There is no reason for you to quarrel with the lawyer you are discharging. Nor is it necessary for you to explain your actions. It's your decision.

# CHAPTER XII

# Pitfalls of the
Do-It-Yourself Divorce

## A. When You Can Be Your Own Lawyer

You may have noticed that throughout this book I have continually advised you to consult your lawyer. I have suggested when you should consult your lawyer, what you should tell your lawyer, and how you should work with your lawyer. You may, therefore, have concluded that I think it's a good idea to have a lawyer when you get a divorce. I do.

Now, you have probably seen and read one of the numerous articles about do-it-yourself divorce. I don't recommend this chancy procedure any more than a dentist would suggest you pull your own tooth or an oculist would send you to the dime store for a pair of glasses.

I will, however, present a checklist of a situation in which do-it-yourself divorce could operate. Read the list and if you score 100 per cent you can give it a try.

1. If you live in a state where there are no-fault grounds (incompatibility, living separate and apart, irreconcilable differences) and you intend to use no-fault grounds;
2. If the procedures for obtaining a divorce in your state are relatively simple;
3. If your marriage was of short duration (under five years);
4. If there are no children;
5. If there is little property to divide;
6. If the family debts are easy to assume or to pay;
7. If your wife doesn't want alimony;
8. If both of you want the divorce;
9. If both of you are in agreement as to how to divide the property.

## B. Retake the Test

If you didn't qualify in all of the categories, you are in need of a lawyer. Go back over the factors and let me point out why. Taking the factors one at a time:

1. If you live in a state where fault is still the basis for obtaining a divorce, ask yourself these questions: Can your wife accuse you of adultery? Can she accuse you of cruelty? You need to know what and how to answer. Can you prove misconduct on her part?

Do the traditional defenses to divorce still persist in your state—condonation, collusion, and recrimination? You would be totally at a loss without a lawyer if such defenses were to be raised against you.

2. As we have discussed, divorce procedures are

often confusing to the layman. Would you be wasting more time in learning the procedures than the effort is worth?

3. If your marriage was for some length of time (over five years), doubtless you have acquired both property and debts. These are hard to untangle. You may have intangible property interests that have been building up over the years. Your pension and retirement fund is property. If you don't protect yourself, your ex-wife may later lay claim to part of it.

If you were your own lawyer, would you have thought of the intangibles? Would you know how to protect yourself in regard to them? A long marriage may create rights for your wife that you don't know or think about in pension, Social Security and other benefits.

4. Children create problems. Custody is only one of them. How about visitation? Are you satisfied that visitation will not be a problem? And what about child support? You and your wife might agree *now* on child support, but how shall the extraordinary expenses in the future be handled? What about medical insurance? Suppose you should die while the children are minors? Have you thought about life insurance for them or how to protect your second wife and children from the claims of the first?

5. If you do have substantial property, you need legal advice. You don't have to be a millionaire for your property to be considered substantial. If you own a service station, a dry cleaning establishment, a hardware store, a plumbing-supply house, an auto repair shop, a grocery store, a pharmacy, a clothing store—any kind of business, large or small—you

need legal advice in a divorce action. If you don't have sound advice you might have your wife for a permanent partner in business.

6. If the debts are substantial (whose aren't?), you should have legal advice on the best way to handle them.

7. If your wife wants and needs alimony, you should have legal advice as to how much to pay. You should be acquainted with all tax consequences of alimony.

8. If your wife doesn't want the divorce, you are thrown back to the issue of grounds—fault, and defenses to divorce. In handling these questions you are surely going to need a lawyer. You need to know how to proceed on your own.

9. If you and your wife can't agree on the property and debt division, you have no choice but to seek the counsel of a lawyer.

## C. Where a Lawyer Saves You Money

As I have indicated, future problems may arise that could have been avoided if the parties had consulted a lawyer before their divorce. One area is the often overlooked intangible properties. The most obvious example of these are pension and retirement funds and rights.

Debts division is another problem area. Your creditors are not bound by the decision that you and your wife make. They want their money. If your wife agreed to pay and doesn't, you are stuck. A lawyer could have foreseen the possibility and protected you.

As we have stated, there are federal income tax

consequences to alimony and property division. The IRS may question these arrangements years later. Did you remember to provide for this possibility when you acted as your own lawyer?

If you die while your children are still minors, they have a claim against your estate for support. Your wife may also. Did you provide for these possibilities when you acted as your own lawyer?

The foregoing are just a few of the problems that can arise. Keep these in mind when you are tempted to act as your own lawyer. We have an old adage in the law that goes like this: "He who represents himself has a fool for a client."

There are many sound ways to economize in life. Acting as your own attorney is rarely one of them.

# Appendix A

## ALABAMA

**Residence:** Six months with exceptions.

**Grounds:**
1. Physically and incurably incapacitated from entering into the marriage state.
2. Adultery.
3. Voluntary abandonment for one year.
4. Imprisonment for two years.
5. Conviction of crime against nature.
6. Habitual drunkenness or habitual use of drugs
7. Incompatibility.
8. Incurable insanity.
9. Irretrievable breakdown of the marriage.

**Alimony:** Available to wife.

**Property Division:** Each keeps his separate property although the court may award wife part of husband's property by way of alimony for the wife.

## ALASKA

| | |
|---|---|
| *Residence:* | Requirement held unconstitutional. |
| *Grounds:* | 1. Impotency. |
| | 2. Adultery. |
| | 3. Conviction of a felony. |
| | 4. Willful desertion for one year. |
| | 5. Cruel and inhuman treatment. |
| | 6. Personal indignities. |
| | 7. Incompatibility of temperament. |
| | 8. Habitual drunkenness. |
| | 9. Incurable mental illness. |
| | 10. Addiction to drugs. |
| *Alimony:* | Available to either spouse. |
| *Property Division:* | As court deems just. |

## ARIZONA

| | |
|---|---|
| *Residence:* | Ninety days. |
| *Grounds:* | Marriage irretrievably broken down. |
| *Alimony:* | Available to either spouse. |
| *Property Division:* | Community property divided without regard to marital misconduct. |

## ARKANSAS

| | |
|---|---|
| *Residence:* | Sixty days. |
| *Grounds:* | 1. Impotency. |
| | 2. Desertion for one year. |
| | 3. Prior existing marriage. |
| | 4. Conviction of a felony. |
| | 5. Habitual drunkenness. |
| | 6. Adultery. |
| | 7. Living separate and apart for three years. |
| | 8. Incurable insanity. |

|  | 9. Cruelty. |
| *Alimony:* | Available to wife. |
| *Property Division:* | Wife entitled to one third of husband's personal property and one third of his lands for life. |

## CALIFORNIA

| *Residence:* | Six months. |
| *Grounds:* | 1. Incurable insanity. |
|  | 2. Irreconcilable differences. |
| *Alimony:* | Available to either spouse. |
| *Property Division:* | Community property divided evenly without regard to fault. Separate property remains property of spouse acquiring it. |

## COLORADO

| *Residence:* | Ninety days. |
| *Grounds:* | Irretrievable breakdown of marriage. |
| *Alimony:* | Available as maintenance for either spouse. |
| *Property Division:* | Marital property divided as court deems just, without regard to misconduct; contribution of each spouse (including contribution as homemaker) to the marital property and other factors are considered. |

## CONNECTICUT

| *Residence:* | One year with exceptions. |
| *Grounds:* | 1. Irretrievable breakdown of marriage. |
|  | 2. Living separate and apart for |

eighteen months.
3. Adultery.
4. Fraud.
5. Desertion for a year.
6. Seven years' absence.
7. Habitual intemperance.
8. Intolerable cruelty.
9. Sentence to imprisonment for life.
10. Conviction of infamous crime involving a violation of conjugal duty and punishable by imprisonment for more than one year.
11. Legal confinement because of mental illness for an accumulated period of at least five years.

*Alimony:* Available to either spouse.
*Property Division:* As court deems just.


## DELAWARE

*Residence:* Three months.
*Grounds:*
1. Marriage irretrievably broken because of separation.
2. Incompatibility.
3. Respondent's mental illness or misconduct, including:
   a. Adultery
   b. Conviction of a crime.
   c. Desertion.
   d. Homosexuality.
   e. Lesbianism.
   f. Venereal disease
   g. Excessive use of liquor or drugs or serious offenses

involving the same.

| | |
|---|---|
| *Alimony:* | Available to respondent only. |
| *Property Division:* | Equal division of marital property without regard to misconduct. |

## FLORIDA

| | |
|---|---|
| *Residence:* | Six months. |
| *Grounds:* | 1. Irretrievable breakdown of marriage. |
| | 2. Spouse adjudged mentally incompetent for preceding period of at least three years. |
| *Alimony:* | Available to either spouse. |
| *Property Division:* | Before wife can be awarded property of husband, she must show a special equity interest; obtaining an award of property is considered alimony. |

## GEORGIA

| | |
|---|---|
| *Residence:* | Six months. |
| *Grounds:* | 1. Incest. |
| | 2. Mental incapacity at time of marriage. |
| | 3. Impotency at time of marriage. |
| | 4. Force, menace, duress, fraud. |
| | 5. Pregnancy at time of marriage unknown to husband. |
| | 6. Conviction of offense involving moral turpitude where penalty is punishable by two years or more in state penitentiary. |
| | 7. Adultery. |
| | 8. Desertion. |
| | 9. Habitual intoxication. |
| | 10. Cruelty. |

11. Incurable mental illness.
12. Habitual addiction to drugs.
13. Irretrievably broken marriage.
Available to wife.

*Alimony:*
*Property Division:* Each keeps his separate property although the court may set aside part of husband's property by way of alimony for wife.

## HAWAII

*Residence:* One Year.

*Grounds:*
1. Marriage irretrievably broken.
2. Living separate and apart for two years.

*Alimony:* Available to either spouse.

*Property Division:* The court may divide the property in any manner it deems just.

## IDAHO

*Residence* Six weeks.

*Grounds*
1. Adultery.
2. Extreme cruelty.
3. Willful desertion.
4. Willful neglect.
5. Habitual intemperance.
6. Conviction of felony.
7. Permanent insanity.
8. Living separate and apart for five years.
9. Irreconcilable differences.

*Alimony:* Allowed to wife for fault of husband.

*Property Division:* Community-property state. Division as may be just.

## ILLINOIS

| | |
|---|---|
| *Residence:* | Six months if offense occurred in state; otherwise one year. |
| *Grounds:* | 1. Impotency at time of marriage. |
| | 2. Adultery. |
| | 3. Desertion for one year. |
| | 4. Habitual drunkenness for two years. |
| | 5. Attempt on life of spouse by means showing malice. |
| | 6. Extreme and repeated mental or physical cruelty. |
| | 7. Conviction of a felony or other infamous crime. |
| | 8. Communication of a venereal disease. |
| | 9. Excessive use of addictive drugs for two years. |
| *Alimony:* | Available to either spouse. |
| *Property Division:* | On equitable terms as court deems just. |

## INDIANA

| | |
|---|---|
| *Residence:* | Six months. |
| *Grounds:* | 1. Irretrievable breakdown of marriage. |
| | 2. Conviction of infamous crime. |
| | 3. Impotency existing at time of marriage. |
| | 4. Incurable insanity for two years. |
| *Alimony:* | Parties may agree to alimony. |
| *Property Division:* | Divided in just and reasonable manner as determined by court. |

## IOWA

| | |
|---|---|
| *Residence:* | One Year. |
| *Grounds* | Breakdown of marriage to extent of legitimate objects of matrimony have been destroyed. |
| *Alimony:* | Available to either spouse. |
| *Property Division:* | Division as may be just. |

## KANSAS

| | |
|---|---|
| *Residence:* | Sixty days. |
| *Grounds:* | 1. Abandonment for one year. |
| | 2. Adultery. |
| | 3. Extreme cruelty. |
| | 4. Habitual drunkenness. |
| | 5. Gross neglect of marital duty. |
| | 6. Conviction of a felony and imprisonment thereof subsequent to the marriage. |
| | 7. Confinement for three years because of mental illness, or adjudication of mental illness by a court for three years. |
| | 8. Incompatibility. |
| *Alimony:* | Available to either party. |
| *Property Division:* | As may be just. |

## KENTUCKY

| | |
|---|---|
| *Residence:* | 180 days. |
| *Grounds:* | Irretrievable breakdown of marriage relationship. |
| *Alimony:* | Available to either spouse. |
| *Property Division:* | As may be just. Fault may still be a factor in property division. |

## LOUISIANA

*Residence:* None.

*Grounds:*
1. Adultery.
2. Conviction of a felony and sentences to death or imprisonment at hard labor.
3. Separation by party who obtained decree and one year elapsed without reconciliation.
4. If separation decreed, by either party after two years.
5. Separation decree may be obtained for the following additional grounds:
   a. Habitual intemperance.
   b. Cruelty.
   c. Defamation.
   d. Abandonment.
   e. Attempt on life of spouse.
   f. Other spouse charged with felony and fled state.
   g. Intentional nonsupport.
   h. Voluntary living separate and apart for one year.

*Alimony:* Available to wife.

*Property Division:* Equal division of community property.


## MAINE

*Residence:* Six months with certain exceptions.

*Grounds:*
1. Adultery.
2. Impotence.
3. Extreme cruelty.
4. Desertion for three years.

211

| | |
|---|---|
| | 5. Habitual use of liquor or drugs. |
| | 6. Cruelty. |
| | 7. Irreconcilable marital differences. |
| | 8. Failure to support. |
| *Alimony:* | Available to wife. |
| *Property Division:* | Wife is entitled to a portion of husband's real estate. |

## MARYLAND

| | |
|---|---|
| *Residence:* | One year with exceptions. |
| *Grounds:* | 1. Impotency existing at time of marriage. |
| | 2. Any cause rendering marriage void *ab initio* under Maryland law. |
| | 3. Adultery. |
| | 4. Abandonment for twelve months. |
| | 5. Voluntary separation for twelve months. |
| | 6. Conviction of felony or misdemeanor and sentenced to imprisonment for three years or indeterminate time. |
| | 7. Uninterrupted separation for three years. |
| | 8. Incurable insanity. |
| *Alimony:* | Available to wife. |
| *Property Division:* | Wife may be awarded her property. Division of marital personal property may be made, but real property acquired solely from contribution of one spouse may not be awarded to the other. |

212

## MASSACHUSETTS

| | |
|---|---|
| *Residence:* | Divorce action may be brought only by bona fide domiciliary of state. |
| *Grounds:* | 1. Adultery.<br>2. Impotence.<br>3. Desertion.<br>4. Habitual and excessive use of drugs or liquor.<br>5. Cruelty.<br>6. Failure to support.<br>7. Sentence and confinement in penal institution for five years. |
| *Alimony:* | Available to either spouse. |
| *Property Division:* | Marital rights cease. Jointly owned property not affected. Court may order division of property in conjunction with alimony. |

## MICHIGAN

| | |
|---|---|
| *Residence:* | One year with exceptions. |
| *Grounds:* | Breakdown of marriage to extent that objects of matrimony have been destroyed. |
| *Alimony:* | Available to either spouse. |
| *Property Division:* | As court deems just. |

## MINNESOTA

| | |
|---|---|
| *Residence:* | One year. |
| *Grounds:* | Irretrievable breakdown of the marriage. |
| *Alimony:* | Available to either spouse. |
| *Property Division:* | Division of marital property as is just. In addition, court may award to either up to one half of the property of the other spouse. |

## MISSISSIPPI

*Residence:* One year plus bona fide residence.

*Grounds:*
1. Natural impotency.
2. Adultery.
3. Sentence to penitentiary.
4. Desertion for one year.
5. Habitual and excessive use of drugs or liquor.
6. Cruelty.
7. Insanity.
8. Prior existing marriage.
9. Consanguinity without prohibited degrees.

*Alimony:* Available to wife.

*Property Division:* Jointly owned property not affected.

Marital rights cease. Separate property of each not affected.

## MISSOURI

*Residence:* Ninety days.

*Grounds:* Irretrievable breakdown of marriage.

*Alimony:* Available to either spouse.

*Property Division:* Marital property divided as court deems just.

## MONTANA

*Residence:* One year.

*Grounds:*
1. Adultery.
2. Extreme cruelty.
3. Willful desertion.
4. Conviction of a felony.
5. Habitual intemperance.
6. Irreconcilable differences.
7. Willful neglect.

8. Incurable insanity.

*Alimony:* Available to wife only. If husband obtains the divorce, not available to the wife.

*Property Division:* Separate property of each not affected. Innocent party may have homestead in property of the other.

## NEBRASKA

*Residence:* One year.

*Grounds:* Irretrievable breakdown of marriage.

*Alimony:* Available to either spouse.

*Property Division:* As court deems just.

## NEVADA

*Residence:* Six weeks with exceptions.

*Grounds:*
1. Insanity for two years prior to commencement of action.
2. Living separate and apart for one year.
3. Incompatibility.

*Alimony:* Available to wife.

*Property Division:* Community property divided as court deems just. Separate property of husband may be set apart for wife's support.

## NEW HAMPSHIRE

*Residence:* One year with exceptions.

*Grounds:*
1. Impotency.
2. Extreme cruelty.
3. Conviction and imprisonment for more than one year.
4. Adultery.

5.  Absence for two years and not heard from.
6.  Habitual drunkenness for two years.
7.  Joining any religious sect which professes to believe relation of husband and wife unlawful and refusal to cohabit for six months.
8.  Abandonment and refusal to cohabit for two yeras.
9.  Absence without consent of other for two years.
10. Various other forms of abandonment.

*Alimony:*          Available to wife.
*Property Division:* Division as court deems just.


NEW JERSEY

*Residence:*        One year with exceptions.
*Grounds:*
1.  Adultery.
2.  Desertion for twelve months.
3.  Extreme cruelty.
4.  Living separate and apart for eighteen months.
5.  Addiction to alcohol or drugs.
6.  Institutionalization for mental illness.
7.  Imprisonment for crime for eighteen months.
8.  Deviate sexual conduct without consent of other.

*Alimony:*          Available to either spouse.
*Property Division:* Division as court deems equitable.

## NEW MEXICO

*Residence:* Six months.
*Grounds:*
1. Adultery.
2. Cruelty.
3. Abandonment.
4. Incompatibility.

*Alimony:* Available to either spouse.
*Property Division:* Division as court deems just.


## NEW YORK

*Residence:* Two years with exceptions.
*Grounds:*
1. Cruelty.
2. Abandonment for one year.
3. Imprisonment of defendant for three consecutive years after marriage.
4. Adultery.
5. Living separate and apart for a period of one year pursuant to a separation judgment.
6. Living separate and apart pursuant to a written separation agreement.

*Alimony:* Available to wife.
*Property Division:* When wife secures the divorce, all property owned by her, or personal property in her possession, is divested of husband's interest. Her dower interest in husband's property is not affected by the divorce. Guilty party has no interest in other's life insurance, with exceptions.

## NORTH CAROLINA

| | |
|---|---|
| *Residence:* | Six months. |
| *Grounds:* | 1. Adultery. |
| | 2. Natural impotence at time of marriage. |
| | 3. Pregnancy of wife by another at time of marriage without knowledge of husband. |
| | 4. Continuous separation for one year. |
| | 5. Separation for three years by reason of incurable insanity. |
| | 6. Crime against nature. |
| | 7. Bestiality. |
| *Alimony:* | Available under limited conditions. |
| *Property Division:* | The court may give wife a lifetime right to part of husband's real estate by way of alimony for wife. The court may also order personal property transferred to wife by way of alimony. |

## NORTH DAKOTA

| | |
|---|---|
| *Residence:* | One year with exceptions. |
| *Grounds:* | 1. Adultery. |
| | 2. Extreme cruelty. |
| | 3. Willful desertion. |
| | 4. Willful neglect. |
| | 5. Habitual intemperance. |
| | 6. Conviction for a felony. |
| | 7. Incurable insanity. |
| | 8. Irreconcilable differences. |
| *Alimony:* | Available to either spouse. |
| *Property Division:* | As court deems equitable. |

## OHIO

| | |
|---|---|
| *Residence:* | Six months. |
| *Grounds:* | 1. Prior existing and undissolved marriage. |
| | 2. Willful absence for one year. |
| | 3. Adultery. |
| | 4. Impotency. |
| | 5. Extreme cruelty. |
| | 6. Fraudulent contract. |
| | 7. Gross neglect of duty. |
| | 8. Habitual drunkenness. |
| | 9. Imprisonment in penitentiary. |
| | 10. Procurement of divorce outside state by other party. |
| | 11. Living separate and apart for two years. |
| | 12. Parties' agreement to dissolution. |
| *Alimony:* | Available to either spouse. |
| *Property Division:* | Divorce terminates wife's dower rights. Each receives his separate property. Property may be awarded to other party as alimony. |

## OKLAHOMA

| | |
|---|---|
| *Residence:* | Six months. |
| *Grounds:* | 1. Abandonment for one year. |
| | 2. Adultery. |
| | 3. Impotency. |
| | 4. Pregnancy by other than husband at time of marriage. |
| | 5. Extreme cruelty. |
| | 6. Fraudulent contract. |
| | 7. Incompatibility. |

219

|  | 8. Habitual drunkenness. |
|---|---|
|  | 9. Gross neglect of duty. |
|  | 10. Imprisonment for felony. |
|  | 11. Procurement by other party of divorce outside the state. |
|  | 12. Insanity and confinement for five years. |
| *Alimony:* | Allowable to wife and to husband for child support. |
| *Property Division:* | As court deems just. |

## OREGON

| *Residence:* | Six months with exceptions. |
|---|---|
| *Grounds:* | Irreconcilable differences. |
| *Alimony:* | Available to either spouse. |
| *Property Division:* | Community-property state. Divided as court deems just. |

## PENNSYLVANIA

| *Residence:* | One year. |
|---|---|
| *Grounds:* | 1. Incapability of procreation. |
|  | 2. Prior existing marriage. |
|  | 3. Adultery. |
|  | 4. Desertion for two years. |
|  | 5. Cruel treatment. |
|  | 6. Indignities. |
|  | 7. Uncondoned fraud, force or coercion. |
|  | 8. Conviction of crime resulting in sentence for two years. |
|  | 9. Consanguinity and affinity. |
|  | 10. Insanity and confinement for three years. |
| *Alimony:* | Allowed only where spouse is insane. |
| *Property Division:* | Equal division for most purposes. |

# RHODE ISLAND

| | |
|---|---|
| *Residence:* | Must be bona fide resident. |
| *Grounds:* | 1. Impotency. |
| | 2. Adultery. |
| | 3. Extreme cruelty. |
| | 4. Willful desertion. |
| | 5. Continual drunkenness. |
| | 6. Habitual use of drugs. |
| | 7. Willful neglect. |
| | 8. Living separate and apart for five years. |
| | 9. Any ground for annulment. |
| *Alimony:* | Allowable to wife for fault of husband. |
| *Property Division:* | Claim of alimony is a waiver of dower right. Wife may have dower as if husband dead if husband at fault. If wife is at fault, husband has right to curtesy as if wife is dead. Spouse at fault loses all dower or curtesy rights. Parties have no other right in each other's separate property except wife's right to alimony. |

# SOUTH CAROLINA

| | |
|---|---|
| *Residence:* | One year. |
| *Grounds:* | 1. Adultery. |
| | 2. Desertion for one year. |
| | 3. Physical cruelty. |
| | 4. Separation for three years. |
| | 5. Habitual drunkenness or habitual use of drugs. |
| *Alimony:* | Allowable to nonadulterous wife. |
| *Property Division:* | Wife's dower rights barred by divorce. |

| | |
|---|---|
| *Property Division:* | Separate proeprty of each not affected. |

## SOUTH DAKOTA

| | |
|---|---|
| *Residence:* | Bona fide resident. |
| *Grounds:* | 1. Adultery. |
| | 2. Extreme cruelty. |
| | 3. Willful desertion. |
| | 4. Willful neglect. |
| | 5. Habitual intemperance. |
| | 6. Conviction of a felony. |
| | 7. Incurable insanity. |
| *Alimony:* | Allowable to wife where husband is at fault. |
| *Property Division:* | Equitable division as court deems just. |

## TENNESSEE

| | |
|---|---|
| *Residence:* | Six months, with exceptions. |
| *Grounds:* | 1. Impotency at time of marriage. |
| | 2. Prior existing marriage. |
| | 3. Adultery. |
| | 4. Desertion for one year. |
| | 5. Conviction of an infamous crime. |
| | 6. Conviction of a felony and imprisonment. |
| | 7. Attempt on life of other. |
| | 8. Refusal of wife to live with husband in state and absenting herself for two years. |
| | 9. Pregnancy by another at time of marriage. |
| | 10. Habitual drunkenness or abuse of narcotic drugs. |
| *Alimony:* | Allowable to wife. |
| *Property Division:* | Division as court deems just. |

## TEXAS

| | |
|---|---|
| *Residence:* | One year. |
| *Grounds:* | 1. Cruelty. |
| | 2. Abandonment for one year. |
| | 3. Adultery. |
| | 4. Living separate and apart for three years. |
| | 5. Conviction of a felony and imprisonment. |
| | 6. Confinement to mental institution for five years. |
| | 7. Where marriage has become unsupportable because of conflict in personalities. |
| *Alimony:* | No permanent alimony. |
| *Property Division:* | Division as court deems just. |

## UTAH

| | |
|---|---|
| *Residence:* | Three months. |
| *Grounds:* | 1. Impotency at time of marriage. |
| | 2. Adultery. |
| | 3. Willful desertion for one year. |
| | 4. Willful neglect. |
| | 5. Habitual drunkenness. |
| | 6. Conviction of a felony. |
| | 7. Cruelty. |
| | 8. Permanent insanity legally adjudged. |
| | 9. Separation for three years under decree of separation. |
| *Alimony:* | Available to either spouse. |
| *Property Division:* | As court deems just. |

## VERMONT

| | |
|---|---|
| *Residence:* | One year. |
| *Grounds:* | 1. Adultery. |
| | 2. Confinement to hard labor in |

the state prison.

3. Intolerant severity.
4. Willful desertion or absence for seven years.
5. Failure to support.
6. Incurable insanity.
7. Living separate and apart.

*Alimony:* Available to either spouse.
*Property Division:* As court deems just.

## VIRGINIA

*Residence:* Six months.
*Grounds:*
1. Adultery.
2. Sodomy.
3. Impotency.
4. Conviction of infamous crime.
5. Willful desertion.
6. Pregnancy by another at time of marriage and unknown to husband.
7. Prostitution of wife before marriage and unknown to husband.
8. Separation for two years.

*Alimony:* Available to wife.
*Property Division:* Property rights of each in other's property are extinguished by divorce.

## WASHINGTON

*Residence:* Must be bona fide resident.
*Grounds:* Irretrievable breakdown of marriage.
*Alimony:* Available to either spouse.
*Property Division:* Community-property state. Court makes division as is just without regard to marital misconduct.

## WEST VIRGINIA

| | |
|---|---|
| *Residence:* | One year. |
| *Grounds:* | 1. Adultery. |
| | 2. Conviction of a felony. |
| | 3. Willful desertion for one year. |
| | 4. Cruel and unkind treatment. |
| | 5. Habitual drunkenness. |
| | 6. Drug addiction. |
| | 7. Separation for two years. |
| | 8. Incurable insanity. |
| *Alimony:* | Available to either spouse. |
| *Property Division:* | Dower rights terminated, but guilty party may be required to set over portion of property to other party. |

## WISCONSIN

| | |
|---|---|
| *Residence:* | Six months. |
| *Grounds:* | 1. Adultery. |
| | 2. Imprisonment for three years. |
| | 3. Willful desertion for one year. |
| | 4. Cruel and inhuman treatment. |
| | 5. Habitual drunkenness. |
| | 6. Voluntary separation for one year. |
| | 7. Separation for one year pursuant to judgment. |
| | 8. Failure to support. |
| | 9. Commitment in mental institution for one year. |
| *Alimony:* | Available to either spouse. |
| *Property Division:* | As court deems just. |

## WYOMING

| | |
|---|---|
| *Residence:* | Sixty days. |
| *Grounds:* | 1. Adultery. |
| | 2. Impotency. |
| | 3. Conviction of a felony and |

sentence to prison.
4. Willful desertion for one year.
5. Habitual drunkenness.
6. Extreme cruelty.
7. Failure to support.
8. Indignities.
9. Vagrancy of husband.
10. Conviction of an infamous crime prior to marriage and unknown to other.
11. Pregnancy of wife by another and unknown to husband.
12. Incurable insanity.
13. Separation for two years with qualifications.

*Alimony:* Available to wife.
*Property Division:* As court deems just.

## DISTRICT OF COLUMBIA

*Residence:* One year.
*Grounds:*
1. Adultery.
2. Desertion for one year.
3. Voluntary separation for one year.
4. Conviction of a felony and imprisonment.
5. Separation for one year pursuant to judgment, divorce available to innocent party.

*Alimony:* Available to wife.
*Property Division:* Court orders apportionment as it deems just.

## PUERTO RICO

*Alimony:* One year.
*Property Division:*
1. Adultery.

226

2. Conviction of a felony.
3. Habitual drunkenness or continual use of drugs.
4. Cruel treatment.
5. Abandonment for one year.
6. Incurable impotency occurring after marriage.
7. Attempt of husband or wife to corrupt their sons or prostitute their daughters and connivance in such corruption or prostitution.
8. Proposal of husband to prostitute his wife.
9. Separation for two years.
10. Incurable insanity.

*Alimony:* Available to wife if she is innocent party.

*Property Division:* Community property distributed as court deems just.

## VIRGIN ISLANDS

*Residence:* Six weeks.

*Grounds:* Breakdown of marriage.

*Alimony:* Available to either.

*Property Division:* Court may order husband to deliver to wife her personal property.

# Appendix B

## GLOSSARY OF LEGAL TERMS

*Absolute divorce:* See *Divorce*.

*Action:* Formal means or method of pursuing and recovering one's rights in a court of justice.

*Adult:* Term applied to one who has become of age as set forth in a statute. In most states this is now eighteen (18) years. For some purposes it may still be twenty-one (21) years.

*Adultery:* Voluntary sexual intercourse of a married person with a person other than the offender's husband or wife.

*Affiant:* A person who makes an affidavit.

*Affidavit:* An oath in writing, sworn before a person legally authorized to administer oaths.

*Affinity:* The connection existing in consequence of marriage between each of the married persons and the kindred of the other.

*Age:* A period of life in which persons become legally competent to perform certain acts or enter into certain contracts which before they were not competent to do or enter into.

*Agreement:* An understanding and intention, between two or more parties, with respect to the effect upon their relative rights and duties of certain past or future acts or performances. The act of two or more persons who unite in expressing a mutual and common purpose, with the view of altering their rights and obligations.

*Alimony:* The allowance made to one spouse (usually the wife) out of the other's estate for the support of the spouse, either during a matrimonial suit or after its termination. It is either temporary or permanent. Temporary alimony is paid during litigation or while the parties are in the process of obtaining a divorce. Permanent alimony is paid after the divorce has been granted. Even when the alimony award after divorce is for a limited period of time, it is still termed permanent alimony.

*Allegation:* A statement made in a pleading.

*Annulment:* An action or proceeding for the termination of a marriage on the ground that for some cause existing at the time of the marriage no valid legal marriage ever existed, even though the marriage may be only voidable at the instance of the injured party.

*Answer:* In a general sense, any pleading which is made to meet a previous pleading, such as a complaint.

*Appeal:* The complaint to a superior court of an injustice done or an error committed by an inferior court whose judgment or decision the superior court is called upon to correct or reverse.

*Appearance:* The coming into court of either of the parties to an action or the coming into court by their attorneys.

*Assign:* To make or set over to another; to transfer—as to assign property or some other interest; to transfer by writing.

*Assignee:* A person to whom an assignment is made.

*Assignment:* A transfer or making over, by one person to another, of any property real or personal, in possession or in action, or of any estate or right therein; the instrument making the transfer.

*Assignor:* The one who makes the assignment.

*Attachment:* A taking or seizure of a person or property by virtue of legal process. The attachment is usually done or performed by the sheriff or marshal.

*Attorney:* An attorney-at-law, an advocate, counsel, or official agent employed in preparing, managing and trying causes in the courts; an officer in a court of justice who is employed by a party in a cause to manage it for him.

*Award:* The judgment or decision made and given by a court respecting the matter in dispute.

*Bar:* The place in court which counselors or advocates occupy while addressing the court or jury.

*Bigamy:* The crime of marrying a second time during the existence of a valid marriage, or of having more wives or husbands than one at the same time.

*Bill of Divorce:* A formal written statement or complaint to a court of justice requesting a divorce.

*Blackmail:* Money extorted from a person by threats of exposure.

*Bona fide:* In good faith.

*Breach:* The breaking or violating of the law, right or duty to another either by commission or omission; the breaking of a contracted duty.

*Burden of proof:* The necessity or duty of proving a fact or facts in dispute between the parties to an action.

*Circumstantial evidence:* Evidence derived from circumstances, as distinguished from direct positive proof.

*Client:* A person who employs or retains an attorney, solicitor, advocate, or counselor to appear for him in court, to advise, assist and defend him in legal proceedings and to act for him in any legal business.

*Cohabit:* To live together as husband and wife.

*Collusion:* In divorce proceedings, collusion is an agreement between husband and wife that one of them shall commit, or appear to have committed, or to represent in court as having committed, acts constituting a cause of divorce, for the purpose of enabling the other to obtain a divorce. A deceitful agreement or compact between two or more persons for the one party to bring an action against the other for some evil purpose, as to defraud a third party of his rights.

*Common law:* The whole body of the law of England as distinguished from the civil and canon laws. The common law is the common jurisprudence of the people of the United States. It was brought with them as colonists from England and established here so far as it was adaptable to our institutions and circumstances.

*Community debts:* Those debts incurred by either husband or wife during their marriage and while they are living together.

*Community property:* Property acquired by either husband or wife during the marriage other than property acquired by gift, devise or descent. Property owned in common by husband and wife as a kind of marital partnership. Eight states have the community-property system.

*Complaint:* An accusation or charge against a person as having committed an alleged injury or offense.

*Condonation:* The forgiveness by a husband or wife of a breach of marital duties on the part of the other.

*Consanguinity:* Kindred or alliance in blood. Relation by blood as distinguished from affinity, which is

231

relation by marriage.

*Consideration:* The inducement to a contract, the cause, motive, price or any compelling influence which induces a contracting party to enter into a contract. A reason or material cause of a contract; without consideration a contract is not binding.

*Contempt:* A willful disregard of the authority of a court of justice or legislative body, or disobedience to its lawful orders.

*Contract:* An agreement, upon sufficient consideration, to do or not to do a particular thing. The writing which contains the agreement of the parties.

*Convey:* To pass or transmit the title to property from one to another.

*Costs:* The expenses which are incurred either in the prosecution or defense of an action, or any other proceedings at law.

*Cross-examination:* The examination of a witness by the party opposed to the party who has first examined him, in order to test the truth of such first, or direct, examination.

*Cruelty:* In the law of divorce, that which constitutes grounds for the injured party to obtain a divorce.

*Curtesy:* At common law, the interest to which a man is entitled to his wife's estate upon her death.

*Decree:* The judgment of a court of equity. See also *Judgment.*

*Deed:* A writing under seal containing a conveyance of property between two or more parties.

*Defendant:* The party against whom an action at law is brought.

*Defense:* A denial by the defendant in an action at law of the truth or validity of the plaintiff's complaint.

*Deponent:* One who deposes; one who gives under oath testimony which is reduced to writing.

*Depose:* To state or testify under oath in writing.

*Deposition:* The testimony of a witness under oath taken down in writing before a judicial officer and in answer to interrogatories.

*Desertion:* In divorce, an actual abandonment or breaking off of matrimonial cohabitation, by either of the parties, and a renouncing or refusal of the duties and obligations of the relation, with an intent to abandon or forsake entirely, and not to return to or resume marital relations, occurring without legal justification either in the consent or the wrongful conduct of the other party.

*Dissolution of marriage:* See *Divorce.*

*Divorce:* The legal dissolution of the marriage of a man and a woman, sometimes called absolute divorce as opposed to the English ecclesiastical divorce, called divorce *a mensa et thoro,* which was a partial divorce and which today we would call a legal separation. Divorce *vinculo matrimoni* is a total or absolute divorce of husband and wife as opposed to a divorce *a mensa et thoro.*

*Domicile:* That place where a person has his fixed and permanent home and principal establishment and to which, whenever he is absent, he has the intention of returning. Generally synonymous with residence.

*Dower:* At common law, the interest a wife had in her husband's estate at his death.

*Equity:* The law that grew up in the English Courts of Equity. In its broadest and most general significance, this term denotes the spirit and the habit of fairness, justice and right dealing, which should regulate the intercourse of men with men. The rule of doing to others as we desire them to do to us; also the right of a landowner, in land, over and above the value of the mortgage or loan thereon.

*Equitable:* Just, fair, conformable to the principles of justice and right.

*Evidence:* Any kind of proof or matter legally presented at the trial of an issue by one of the parties through witnesses, documents, records or concrete objects for the purpose of proving a factual issue that is in dispute.

*Hearsay evidence:* Evidence of what others have been heard to say. Testimony from the relation of third persons.

*Injunction:* Order issued by a court at the request of a party, directed to another party, prohibiting the latter from doing some act which he is threatening or attempting to do. It attempts to restrain the adverse party in a suit from commiting any acts in violation of the plaintiff's rights. Sometimes an injunction will command an act to be done.

*Judgment:* The official decision of a court of justice upon the respective rights and claims of the parties to an action or suit litigated therein and then submitted to the court for its determination. *Judgment of divorce:* The decision of the court terminating the marriage. *Judgment of dissolution of marriage:* same as judgment of divorce. *Judgment of separation* or *Separate maintenance:* the decision of the court authorizing the parties to live separately.

*Personal property:* All property other than land or things attached to land.

*Petition:* An application to a court requesting the court to do something. In divorce cases, a petition for divorce is the same as a complaint for divorce or a bill for divorce.

*Property Settlement Agreement:* The agreement between husband and wife settling their respective property rights and obligations each against the other.

*Real property:* Land, things attached to land, and interests on land of an indefinite duration. The converse of personal property.

*Separate maintenance:* The maintenance of a woman by her husband after an agreement to live separately.

*Separation Agreement:* The agreement between husband and wife to separate, which usually provides for the division of the property and the settling of the property rights and other obligations of each against the other. Often used synonymously with *Property Settlement Agreement.*

*Statute:* A law enacted by a legislative body, as opposed to the common law or the law as enunciated by courts in deciding cases.

*Summons (Writ of Summons):* A notice to the defendant that an action against him has been commenced and that judgment will be taken against him if he fails to answer the complaint.

*Writ:* A judicial instrument by which a court commands some act to be done by the person to whom it is directed.

# INDEX

237

238

244

## PRIME TIME
**James Kearney**

LB499-2 $1.95
Novel

The book that picks up where *Network* left off . . . The explosive novel of violent power struggles inside a giant television network. The United Television Network. Outside an austere glass facade . . . inside a seething hot bed of ambitious men and women whose motto was "show your rivals no mercy" . . . men and women who would get what they wanted at any cost. (Foil cover)

## FLAME IN A HIGH WIND
**Jacqueline Kidd**

LB500-X $1.50
Adventure

A Powerful novel of romance and adventure on the high seas. The War of 1812 ended for all but Capt. Denny Poynter. Branded pirate, pursued by British and Americans alike, he fought and plundered his way around the world. But his reckless freedom would be soon jeopardized as his first lady, the sea, gave way to the fiery Renee.

## THAT COLLISION WOMAN
**Deidre Stiles**

LB501-8 $1.95
Novel

Fleur Collison was known as the most beautiful and wilful woman in all England. The young English-woman would return to her ancestral home of Ravensweir despite the fact that it was inhabited by her former lover, now brother-in-law. She was determined to take what she wanted from the world . . . and her sister.

## ELENA
**Emily Francis**

LB502-6 $1.50
Mystery

The commune on this small Greek island lived a placid life among ancient monuments and clear blue sea until Elena came. They gave her friendship and love. She brought them death.

## HOW TO DIVORCE
## YOUR WIFE
**Forden Athearn**

LB503-4 $1.95
Nonfiction

Practical advice for men from an experienced divorce lawyer, Forden Athearn on what to do before you tell your wife, how to tell your wife, family, boss, how to select a lawyer, and more!

## DAY OF THE COMANCHEROS LB504-2 $1.50
**Steven C. Lawrence** Western

Slattery had witnessed the rape, murder, and pillage by the savage Comancheros but it wasn't personal until they put him on the end of a rope. No one dared stop them. Someone had to.

## KILLER SEE, KILLER DO
**Jonathan Wolfe**

LB505-0 $1.50
Mystery

It started out as an innocent Halloween party. But innocent soon turned to bizarre when the treats stopped and a trick involving voodoo brought death to the scene. Someone was jailed and Indian detective Ben Club meant to set him free.

## GUNSMOKE
**Wade Hamilton**

LB506-9 $1.50
Western

Ben Corcoran had become boss of Sageville range by killing anyone who tried to settle. When the quiet gambler came to town no one took notice . . . until he led the farmers in bloody revolt. First Time in Paperback.

## THE LIFE OF KIT CARSON
### John S.C. Abbott
**LB474ZK    $1.25**
**Golden West Series**

Christopher "Kit" Carson was a legend to his countrymen. Trapper, trailblazer, scout, and Indian fighter, Kit Carson would become part of American history at its most exciting time—the pioneering of the wild west.

## THE YOKE AND
## THE STAR
### Tana de Gamez
**LB475TK    $1.95**
**Novel**

"This tense, compassionate novel has an animal warmth and female ferocity that is very moving indeed."

*—Kirkus Review*

"Expert story-telling, excitement and suspense."
*—Publishers Weekly*

Cuba was ready to explode into bloody revolution. Hannan, the American newsman, could feel the tension in the air, in the eyes of the people in the streets and cafes. Everybody was taking sides; there could be no neutrals in the coming conflict. Hannan thought he could stay out of it. He was wrong. Love for a beautiful revolutionary pushed him past the point of no return.

## THE RETURN OF
## JACK THE RIPPER
### Mark Andrews
**LB476KK    $1.75**
**Novel**

An English acting company opened a Broadway play based on the bloody Ripper murders of 1888. Just as the previews began, a prostitute was found dead in a theatre alley—disembowelled, her throat slashed. Other murders followed, and soon the city was gripped in terror. Had the most monstrous figure in the annals of crime returned to kill again?

## THE RED DANIEL
**Duncan MacNeil**

LB477DK   **$1.50**

**Adventure**

The Royal Strathspey's, Britain's finest regiment, are dispatched to South Africa to take command in the bloody Boer War and find the most fabulous diamond in all of South Africa—The Red Daniel.

## SLAVE SHIP
**Harold Calin**

LB478KK   **$1.75**

**Adventure**

This is the story of Gideon Flood, a young romantic who sets sails on a slave ship for a trip that would change his life. He witnesses the cruelty of African chieftains who sell their own for profit, the callousness of the captains who throw the weak overboard, and his own demise as he uses an African slave and then sells her.

## A SPRING OF LOVE
**Celia Dale**

LB479KK   **$1.50**

**Novel**

"A fascinating story."

—*The Washington Star*

"An immaculate performance . . . unsettling, and quite touching."

—*Kirkus Review*

This sweeping novel chronicles a determined young woman's search for enduring love. No matter where it took her, she followed her heart. The man with whom she linked her fortunes was said to be dangerous, but she knew there could be no one else.

## TIME IS THE SIMPLEST THING
**Clifford D. Simak**

LB480DK   **$1.50**

**Science Fiction**

Millions of light years from Earth, the Telepathic Explorer found his mind possessed by an alien creature. Blaine was a man capable of projecting his mind millions of years into time and space. But that awesome alien penetrated his brain, and Blaine turned against the world . . . and himself.

**A PASSION FOR HONOR**     LB467KK    $1.75
Louise MacKendrick                 Nonfiction

Jackson Devereaux had nothing but his rifle and a powerful sense of mission when he came out of the Everglades determined never to return. They called him "swamp-trotter" and other names—but never to his face. Because to insult him was to ask for sudden death. "King Jack" built his private kingdom, sired sons and daughters, but that was only the beginning. For when a man is king there are those who seek to topple him from his throne.

**PLEASURE IS OUR
BUSINESS**                 LB468KK    $1.75
Jack Sandberg                      Nonfiction

This is an explosive exposé of America's fastest growing, profit-making industry, the *total* relaxation center. Sandberg investigates Manhattan's expensive sex clubs . . . establishments that cater to the needs of the "establishment" . . . bars, restaurants, music, topless and bottomless young women in a variety of decors from the decadence of the Roman Empire to the pageantry and pomp of the Indian mosque. Whether cash or charge, anything could be had for a price.

**BLOODY GRASS**           LB469DK    $1.50
Hobe Gilmore                       Western

The U.S. Cavalry was busy with booze, squaws, and officers' wives. But Redband, the crazed renegade Sioux was on the warpath and would stop at nothing to have revenge on white men . . . and white women.

## TARK AND THE GOLDEN TIDE
**Colum MacConnell**

**LB470DK   $1.50**

**Fantasy**

Usurped heir to the throne of the Tumbling Cliffs, Tark and his mentor Morned the Flea journey from the town of Sorne to the Silver Mountains transporting the coveted blue sapphire that is the fabled gem of luck for the Sornese. This is Tark's journey: past the beasts of the Burning Wood, the pirates of the Shallow Sea, and the Princess of the Silver Mountains. But there, at journey's end he must mount his giant fighting camel and meet his deadliest foe—the usurper Akor-Lut, Warmaster of the Golden Tide.

## BLOOD MONEY
**Aaron Fletcher**

**LB471DK   $1.50**

**Western**

Bounty hunter Jake Coulter is back as he scours the west for outlaws with a price on their heads. Now they would know how it felt to be a hunted animal.

## THE WICKED WYNSLEYS
**Alanna Knight**

**LB472DK   $1.50**

**Gothic**

Mab Wynsley and her young actor fiancé buy a mansion as their future home. Until the marriage she would live there accompanied by her sister . . . but soon the house of hope is smashed and she finds herself, her sister, and her future husband actors on a stage of death.

**Cherry Delight**
## THE DEVIL TO PAY
**Glen Chase**

**LB473DK   $1.50**

**Adventure**

Cherry Delight is sent to France to investigate a cult of devil worshippers—extortionists who murder, rape, and maim for pleasure and profit. The Devil presided over the Black Mass and orgies. But he and his disciples were in for a surprise . . . they had never seen hell until Cherry arrived.

## BOMB SQUAD
**Mark Andrews**

LB453DK   $1.50

Novel

It began. First one small bomb. Then several letter bombs, then subway stations, office buildings, rush hour railway terminals. The reign of terror was on. The terrorists gave one last communique. They had one more bomb . . . a nuclear bomb.

## THE MEN IN
## THE JUNGLE
**Norman Spinrad**

LB454KK   $1.50

Science Fiction

Two space travelers stumble onto a planet ruled for three centuries by cruel and corrupt leaders . . . a planet of murder, slavery, torture and cannabalism . . . a planet ripe for revolution.

## THEY CAN ONLY
## KILL YOU ONCE
**Dan Brennan**

LB455DK   $1.50

Novel

An ex-CIA agent is swept into an underworld scheme that places him between the Irish Republican Army and his former organization. Both want to find him. Both want him dead.

## SILENT ENEMY/
## SUNDANCE
**John Benteen**

LB456ZK   $1.25

Western

Both the Indians and the U.S. Cavalry were being victimized by one crazed Cheyenne. Neither brigades of bluecoats nor tribes of braves could end his reign of terror. They needed to pit one man against one crazed Indian. That man was Sundance.

**SEND TO:** LEISURE BOOK
P.O. Box 270
Norwalk, Connecticut 06852

**Please send me the following titles:**

| Quantity | Book Number | Price |
|----------|-------------|-------|
| _____ | _____ | _____ |
| _____ | _____ | _____ |
| _____ | _____ | _____ |
| _____ | _____ | _____ |

**In the event we are out of stock on any of your
selections, please list alternate titles below.**

| _____ | _____ | _____ |
|----------|----------|----------|
| _____ | _____ | _____ |
| _____ | _____ | _____ |
| _____ | _____ | _____ |

Postage/Handling _____

I enclose . . . . . . _____

FOR U.S. ORDERS, add 35¢ per book to cover cost of postage
and handling. Buy five or more copies and we will pay for
shipping. Sorry no C.O.D.'s.

**FOR ORDERS SENT OUTSIDE THE U.S.A.**
Add $1.00 for the first book and 25¢ for each additional
book. PAY BY foreign draft or money order drawn on a
U.S. bank, payable in U.S. ($) dollars.
☐Please send me a free catalog.

NAME_____
(Please print)

ADDRESS_____

CITY _____ STATE _____ ZIP _____
**Allow Four Weeks for Delivery**